12/17

TRANSPARENT SOAPMAKING

A complete guide to making natural see-through soap

D0981666

Written and Illustrated by Catherine Failor

Illustrations by Catherine Failor
Cover and Text Design by Fran Kievet, Summit Design, Portland, OR
Cover Photograph by Kim Brun, Photogroup Inc., Portland, OR

Copyright© 1997 Catherine Failor

All rights reserved. Except for brief passages quoted in reviews, no part of this publication may be reproduced, stored in a retrieval system, or transmitted in any form, or by any means, electronic, mechanical, photocopying, recording, or otherwise, without the written permission of the publisher.

Every effort was made to insure the accuracy of the information presented in this book. All instructions, processes and recommendations are given without guarantee by the author and Rose City Press, who hereby disclaim any liability for accidents, injuries, losses or damages resulting from the use of this book.

Printed in the United States of America by Gilliland Printing
First Printing, March 1997

Failor, Catherine.
    Transparent soapmaking : a complete guide to making natural see-through soap / written and illustrated by Catherine Failor.
    p. cm.
    Includes bibliographical references and index.
    Preassigned LCCN: 96-93093
    ISBN 0-9656390-0-2

    1. Soap. I. Title.

TP991.F35 1997   668'.124
                                QB197-40047

DEDICATION

This book is for my parents, Robert and Letitia Failor
for their love and support.

~~~~~~~~~~~~~~~~~~~~~~~~~~~~~~~

ACKNOWLEDGEMENTS

Many, many thanks go to my friend Kay Whaley, who has been a constant
source of inspiration, ideas and support throughout the writing of this book.

Many thanks also to Fran Kievet for her patience and unerring sense of
good design. This book is partly hers.

A grateful acknowledgement goes to Elaine White,
for her time and valuable suggestions.

A few years ago, when she started work on **The Natural Soap Book**,
Susan Miller Cavitch called me up for help. What little help I could offer
has been returned many times over through her kind encouragement.
Thanks Susan.

To John Toso at Sappo Hill, my best friend in the soap business.

To Kim Brun and Susan Stafford of Photogroup –
thanks for helping make this book look so beautiful!

Grateful thanks to Trish Anderson for her proofreading and editing.
Trish put the "i" back in saponification.

To the Portland Public Library – I can't count the times I called the reference desk.
What would life be without our libraries?

Many thank yous to all these helpful people:
Clyde Abston, Charlie Schmalz, Luis Spitz, George Whalley, Ed Paladini,
Peter Cade, John Prutsman, Jim Bronner, Ken Peterson and Peter Fox.

~~~~~~~~~~~~~~~~~~~~~~~~~~~~~~~

TABLE OF CONTENTS

TABLE OF CONTENTS

INTRODUCTION

Zilch. That's how much informed, practical information on transparent soapmaking is currently available to the amateur soapmaker. Why? Not because the process requires a PhD in chemistry or exotic and expensive chemical ingredients impossible for the layperson to obtain. It doesn't. **If you can follow a recipe from a cookbook you can make transparent soap, and you don't need to look much further than your supermarket, drug and liquor stores for all the necessary ingredients.**

Opaque soaps have been manufactured for at least two thousand years, but transparent soap is a relative newcomer – the first bars were produced almost an exact 200 years ago. So information regarding its manufacture hasn't been circulating for as long or as widely as information concerning opaque soap. The descriptions which do exist are scanty and often confusing. And as is typical with many manufacturing processes, trade secrecy has constricted the informational flow down to a dribble. It's just not in Neutrogena's or Pear's best interest to publish a detailed treatise on transparent soapmaking.

I was in business five years as a soapmaker before attempting to make transparent soap. It was a bit overwhelming. All of the information pertaining to its manufacture resembled a jigsaw puzzle with half of its pieces missing. But the challenge was there. Several months of trial-and-error experimentation ensued, with most of these batches ending up in the garbage can. There finally came the day when information and observation joined to create the big picture. That's what this book contains – all of the relevance with hopefully none of the confusion.

Soapmaking is a lot like cooking. The ingredients are measured, mixed, heated then poured into pans or molds. If your kitchen contains the basic utensils needed for cooking, you're set. The spoons, whisks, spatulas and pots used to make chicken soup or bake a chocolate cake can be used to make transparent soap. An accurate scale is something you might not have, but that can always be borrowed from a friend or purchased used.

Transparent soap consists of the same base that opaque soap does – animal or vegetable oil combined with lye. Lye usually elicits a strong reaction from the uninitiated. "Lye??? You mean there's **lye** in soap? Lye is a poison!!!" But the chemical world is full of beasts turned beauties – it's just a matter of marrying well. Lye combined with oil is no longer lye and the oil is no longer oil. Soap and glycerin are born.

Transparent soap contains a few things that opaque soap doesn't. These aren't mysterious chemicals with impossible-to-pronounce names. In fact, you're sure to have one of the ingredients sitting on your kitchen table – ordinary granulated sugar. Another additive, 190-proof grain alcohol, or ethanol, might be tucked away in the liquor cabinet. You probably won't have a bottle of glycerin on hand, but it's easily found at most drugstores.

Hopefully this will be enough to dispel any initial queasiness you might have about making transparent soap. After all, every bath and body retail chain on the planet is making it, so why don't you? **I guarantee that handmade transparent soap will feel softer, richer, creamier than any commercial brand on the market.**

CHAPTER

ALL ABOUT SOAP

▶ WHAT IS SOAP?

▶ HOW DOES SOAP CLEAN?

▶ OPAQUE SOAP, TRANSPARENT SOAP

Soapmaking is one of the oldest industries in the world although no one knows just when soap was discovered.

WHAT IS SOAP?

Soap is the by-product of a chemical reaction called saponification. Fatty acids present in either vegetable or animal oils are combined with a strong base, or alkali, namely caustic soda or caustic potash. Sodium-based (soda) soaps are hard; potassium-based (potash) soaps are liquid.

A variety of methods exist for soap manufacture such as full-boiled, semi-boiled and cold-process. Large-scale commercial production is done in enormous steam-heated vats using the full-boiled method. This process allows for the greatest control over the finished product, since any unreacted lye can be removed at the end of the process. Some smaller specialty companies and the home soapmaker use the cold-process method, whereby the heat generated from the reaction of fatty acids and alkalis enables the soap to form. These soaps are usually less neutral than full-boiled soaps since they are more liable to contain both free alkali and unsaponified fats. Transparent soap is made using the semi-boiled method. The oils and caustic solution are combined then heated, though not to the boiling point.

A neutral pH is 7; our skin's pH ranges between 5 and 6.5, which is somewhat acidic. "Neutral" soaps are quite alkaline, with a pH of around 9.5. This wide discrepancy between our skin's pH and the pH of soap explains why so many soaps are drying to the skin.

Saponification is the term used to describe the acid/base chemical reaction which forms soap.

This problem can be somewhat corrected by "superfatting" the soap, or adding an excess of fatty acids or oils. Another process involves both superfatting the sodium soap and at the same time blending it with a soap created from the chemical compound triethanolamine or TEA. The resulting soap is both extremely mild and very rinsible. The inventor referred to this property as "neutrogenous," and that's how Neutrogena soap was born.

HOW DOES SOAP CLEAN?

Soap has been cleansing us for centuries without anyone knowing just how. The answer lies in the molecular structures of water, oil and soap.

Water is a bipolar molecule. One of its ends, two hydrogen atoms, is positively charged; the other end, an oxygen atom, is negatively charged. This bipolar nature gives water a cohesiveness which resists being broken apart; you may have noticed that a drinking glass can be filled with water until the water is actually standing above the rim without overflowing. Water's love for itself makes it particularly incompatible with oil. This is because oil has an electrical charge which is uniform; there are no positive and negative poles to the molecule. What is needed to bring water and oil together is a substance which resembles them both – partly polar, partly non-polar, able to act as an intermediary. *That's what soap is.*

What is needed to bring water and oil together is a substance which resembles them both – that's what soap is.

During saponification, the fatty acids combine with the caustic sodium or potassium to form a soap molecule. One end of this molecule is composed of the water-soluble sodium or potassium group; the other end consists of the water-insoluble fatty acid group. This molecule looks like a snake, with a sodium "head" and fatty acid "tail."

Soap is composed of a water-soluble alkali "head" and a water-insoluble fatty acid "tail."

When soap is added to plain water it doesn't actually dissolve. What happens is that the fatty tails hurry to the surface to avoid contact with the water and align themselves tail-up in the air. This breaks the water's surface tension and causes it to spread. If you take some soap solution and add it to that nearly-overflowing glass of water, it will immediately cause the water to cascade over the rim of the glass.

Soil is usually enveloped in an oily film. When soiled fabric or oils are added to soapy water, the fatty tails of the soap rush to them, seeking to bond with a substance of similar molecular make-up. These tails act as tiny hammers, chipping away at the soil and grease. The grease then balls up into smaller droplets. With the soap's oil-loving tails embedded in the grease and its water-loving sodium heads straining outwards towards the water in the basin, the grease and grime can be washed down the drain.

SOAP MOLECULE

FATTY ACID "TAIL" SODIUM OR POTASSIUM "HEAD"

OPAQUE SOAP, TRANSPARENT SOAP

During part of the soapmaking process all soap passes through a colloidal phase. A colloid is any gel-like insoluble substance made up of particles larger than molecules but small enough so that they remain suspended in a fluid medium without settling to the bottom. If you've ever made soap and peeked at it as it's curing in the molds, you might have noticed that at one point the soap will appear as a translucent gel. This is the colloidal state.

As the soap cools, long fibrous crystals begin developing. They increase in number and length and enmesh with one another; gradually the translucency of the colloidal state disappears and the soap becomes opaque. This is because the increasing number of crystals render the soap impervious to the passage of light waves. These crystals are what give ordinary bar soap its opacity.

Transparent soap is made using the same initial process as opaque soap **but at the point when the soap gels, solvents are added to create transparency.**

Transparent soap is made using the same initial process as opaque soap. But at the point when the soap gels, solvents are added. Glycerin, ethyl alcohol (ethanol) and ordinary table sugar are the solvents which will be used in this book. These solvents hold the soap mass in the colloidal state and suppress development of long crystals. Transparent soap does contain crystals, but they are so exceedingly small that light waves can pass right on through the bar. Transparency is defined as the ability to read a **14-point typeface** through a 1/4" thick sliver of soap.

Because of the presence of these additives, a transparent bar will contain only about 50-60% actual soap. Opaque bars contain approximately 85%. This difference explains just why transparent bars have shorter life spans in your shower and sink. And even though the pH of both transparent and opaque soap is about the same, transparent soap rinses off the skin much more readily. This accounts for its exceptional mildness.

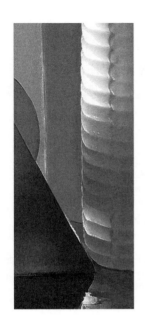

Successful

soapmaking

depends upon

knowing the

characteristics of

the materials you

are working with

and how they

affect one another.

CHAPTER

KNOWING YOUR INGREDIENTS

Most of what we're surrounded with in our lives is so commonplace that we rarely stop to consider just what things really are. This is especially true in the modern industrialized world, since almost all of our material goods are made by a machine or another person, usually thousands of miles away. But whether you're baking bread, glazing pottery or building a cabinet, success always hinges on a knowledge of each material's characteristics and how one material affects another.

Soapmaking is no different. Each fat and oil used to produce a bar of soap has its own unique chemistry which in turn affects the soap's hardness, solubility and lather. Transparent soap contains additional substances such as alcohol, glycerin and sugar which act as solvents and gel-formers. This chapter is intended to deepen your understanding of each ingredient's characteristics, which could be useful for problem-solving or for formulating your own soap.
The Formulating appendix contains charts and further information on soapmaking.

Each fat and oil used to produce a bar of soap has its own unique chemistry which in turn affects the soap's hardness, solubility and lather.

FATS AND OILS

The difference between a fat and an oil is somewhat arbitrary, based upon their physical state at room temperature – fat being solid and oil liquid. *Oils are divided into three classes: mineral oils (derived from petroleum), essential oils (any volatile oil which gives the distinctive fragrance to a plant, flower or fruit) and fixed oils.* **Fixed oils, which are either animal or vegetable in origin, comprise the main raw materials for soapmaking due to their easy reactibility with alkalis.** Specifically, the fatty acids in these oils are what combine chemically with the alkalis; this process is known as saponification. *The fixed oils are further classified as follows:*

Hard Fats

Palm oil and animal tallow are the two most common hard fats used for soapmaking. Hard fats are largely composed of stearin and palmitin, fatty acids which are solid at room temperature and therefore lend firmness to the fats; this firmness however, has the disadvantage of creating soaps which do not readily dissolve in water. *A soap composed exclusively of either palm or tallow will be very brittle with a low, though persistent lather.*

Palm oil is extracted from the fruit pulp of the oil palm and is becoming increasingly difficult to find in this country due to health concerns over saturated fats in our diets. Wholesale bakery or grocery suppliers are the most likely sources for 35-pound pails. *Other sources are listed in the Suppliers appendix.*

Tallow is the fat of cattle or sheep; suet is the fat specifically found surrounding the kidneys of these animals. Tallow and palm can be used interchangeably in soap formulation, although *tallow may possibly worsen skin conditions such as eczema and acne.*

When purchasing oils in larger quantities, it's recommended that you melt all of the oil then stir to homogenize. Cooling oils tend to layer – the harder, less meltable fractions on the bottom; the softer, more meltable fractions on top.

It has been the primary fat used in soapmaking for two millennium and is much easier to obtain than palm. *Simple instructions for rendering tallow are outlined in the Appendices.*

As an alternative to palm and tallow, lard can be used. Lard is rendered pig fat. One big advantage to lard is that you can buy it cheaply in one pound cubes at most grocery stores, already cleaned and refined. *Soap made with lard is a bit softer than palm or tallow-based soap.*

Nut Oils

Coconut oil and palm kernel oil are the most typical nut oils used for soapmaking. Coconut and palm kernel oils are characterized by a large proportion of lauric acid which produces a very soluble and quick-lathering soap. (Not all nut oils, however, have this high percentage of lauric acid.) What is unusual about lauric acid is that it also produces a hard soap; all other oils capable of hardening soap have the disadvantage of poor solubility. *Soaps created exclusively from coconut or palm kernel oil, however, are drying to the skin and though they lather profusely, the lather is short-lived.*

Coconut oil is pressed from dried coconut meat (copra) and palm kernel oil is extracted from the kernel (as opposed to the fruit) of the oil palm. Coconut oil can be purchased at most health food stores; 35-pound pails can also be found at large grocery wholesalers or bakery supply houses.

Soap made with lard is softer than palm or tallow-based soap.

Palm kernel is not as easy to find. *For more information consult the Suppliers appendix.*

Both of these oils have similar soapmaking properties and can be used interchangeably. However, more sodium hydroxide is necessary to saponify coconut oil than is needed for palm kernel. The recipes in this book have been calculated for coconut oil only. *If you wish to use palm kernel oil in place of coconut, consult the Formulating section in the Appendices and recalculate.* Palm kernel requires approximately 80% of the amount of sodium hydroxide needed to saponify coconut oil.

Soft Oils

Unsaturated fatty acids such as oleic and linoleic are the primary components of most soft oils: olive, cottonseed, corn, canola, soy, sesame and peanut are common soft oils. The soapmaking properties of these oils vary according to the proportions of each oil's fatty acid content, but generally soft oils yield thin, long-lasting lathers with good detergent properties. *None of these oils should be used alone for soapmaking, however, as they cannot produce a hard bar.*

Castor oil, a thick, viscous oil extracted from the castor bean, is the traditional soft oil of choice for transparent soapmaking. Castor oil differs from most other soft oils in its fatty acid composition; **80-85% of castor oil is made up of ricinoleic acid. The peculiar nature of this fatty acid gives castor solvent-like properties**, and

Soft oils yield thin long-lasting lathers with good detergent properties.

solvents are what render ordinary soap transparent. *Other soft oils can be substituted for castor oil, but the resulting soap will be somewhat less transparent.*

Castor has the additional virtue of acting as a humectant – it draws and holds moisture from the air to the skin. *Too large a proportion of castor in a recipe, however, makes the finished bar soft and sticky and also reduces its lathering properties.* Castor can be found or ordered from drugstores and health food stores. *Other sources are listed in the back of this book.*

NOTE: *Avoid sulfated castor oil. Sulfated castor is water-soluble which causes an oil blend to "seize" and curdle as soon as the lye solution is added.*

The fatty acid composition of castor oil greatly enhances a soap's transparency.

One of the arts of soapmaking lies in the selection and blending of oils.

Blending Oils

You can see from the above description of oils that any single oil used alone will not produce a satisfactory bar of soap – the soap will be either too hard, too soft, of insufficient lather, etc. One of the arts of soapmaking lies in the selection and blending of oils. **The best soap will consist of coconut or palm kernel oil for firmness and quick foam, a hard fat for firmness but also for stabilizing and extending the life of the lather, and a soft oil for a rich, soluble lather.** *For anyone interested in formulating their own soap, the Appendices contains additional information.*

ALKALIS

The two alkalis used in soap production are **sodium hydroxide, or caustic soda, and potassium hydroxide, or caustic potash.** Soda-based soaps are solid; potash-based soaps are liquid. **Caustic soda will be used for all the transparent soap recipes in this book.**

Commercially, caustic soda is produced by the electrolysis of brine (seawater); the other by-product of this process is chlorine, used for bleaching and water treatment. Caustic soda is most frequently found in either bead or flake form; large soap operations purchase it as a liquid. You can find pure lye in 12-ounce cans in the cleaning section of your local supermarket – look for **Red Devil brand. Don't use Drano.** It's not pure lye. If you plan on making a lot of soap, the cheapest and easiest alternative is a 50-pound bag which can be purchased from chemical wholesalers in your local area. *Other sources for caustic soda are listed in the Suppliers appendix.*

Caustic soda is extremely hygroscopic, or water-loving; a small bead will quickly swell up with atmospheric moisture and become a large droplet. Care must therefore be taken in storing any half-used containers. *Caustic soda is also extremely corrosive – it burns skin within seconds of exposure. Gloves and goggles are a must when handling and mixing lye solutions, and during the mixing of the soap itself.*

Transparent soap is made using caustic soda. Care must be taken when handling this corrosive chemical. Gloves and goggles are a must.

In case of exposure to the skin, always keep a bottle of vinegar or lemon juice handy – the strong acid quickly neutralizes the strong base of lye. This works faster than rinsing with plain water, but don't use vinegar or lemon juice in eyes or in cases where the lye has been ingested. *The rule for caustic soda is the same as that for any hazardous substance – read the warning labels!*

DISTILLED OR SOFT WATER

Whether you're making transparent or opaque soap, water will be mixed with caustic soda to create a lye solution. Transparent soaps require additional water in the form of a sugar solution. *Tap water is not recommended because depending upon where you live, it can contain dissolved salts and other mineral impurities which may impart a cloudiness or "efflorescence," as transparent soapmakers say, to the finished bar of soap.* These salts and minerals act as "seeds" around which other impurities can coalesce, in much the same way as pearls form around grains of sand inside an oyster. **For this reason, distilled or soft water is strongly recommended for transparent soap.**

Water also contributes to the soap's transparency due to its nature as a solvent. Even though much of this water eventually evaporates, the soap retains its transparency.

Water must be free of mineral impurities which can cause cloudiness in transparent soap.

ALCOHOL

Alcohol is the **primary solvent used in transparent soapmaking.** After the initial batch of soap has been mixed and left to sit in the pot for a couple of hours, alcohol is added. With a little stirring, the alcohol dissolves the soap into a clear, amber liquid. Some old soap manuals claim that it's possible to make transparent soap without alcohol – additional glycerin and sugar solution are used instead. But a soap made without alcohol will likely cloud with age.

Ethyl alcohol (or ethanol), more commonly known as 190-proof grain alcohol, is the type of alcohol required for all the recipes in this book. Ethanol, colorless and extremely flammable, is produced by the fermentation of starches, sugars and other carbohydrates. A certain amount of ethanol can be substituted with less expensive isopropyl alcohol. (Isopropyl is prepared from propylene, a gas obtained during the refinement of petroleum.) But because ethanol is a stronger solvent than isopropyl, *soap made using an ethanol/isopropyl blend will be less transparent.*

Ethanol can be found at your local supermarket or liquor store – the most common brand names are Clear Springs and Everclear. When purchasing bottles for soapmaking keep in mind that one fluid pint of alcohol doesn't weigh one pound; alcohol has a lower specific gravity than water. **One pint of alcohol weighs roughly 12.5 ounces.**

Ethanol, or grain alcohol, is the primary solvent used in transparent soapmaking.

Two denatured

alcohols which

are acceptable

for use in soaps

and shampoos

are SDA 3A

and SDA 3C.

Ethanol can also be purchased through scientific and chemical supply houses. *This ethyl alcohol is referred to as "denatured" and it costs considerably less than liquor store ethanol, particularly when purchased by the gallon. The trick is to find it in your local area.* Although some suppliers are listed in the Appendices, shippers such as UPS consider ethanol a hazardous substance owing to its flammability. An extra fee (besides the shipping cost) is consequently added to the denatured alcohol. Its cost may then end up equaling or even exceeding the cost of liquor store ethanol. To source denatured alcohol in your hometown, look in the yellow pages under "Scientific Instruments and Supplies" or "Chemicals."

Ethanol is denatured to make it unfit for drinking or redistillation. Many substances are used as denaturants – essential oils, ketones, vinegar, benzene, bone oil – to name just a few. *Many of these denaturants are either toxic or strong-smelling, making them unsuitable for soapmaking.*

Two denatured alcohols which are acceptable for use in soaps and shampoos are SDA 3A and SDA 3C. SDA stands for "Specially Denatured Alcohol." SDA 3A is composed of 100 parts ethanol to 5 parts methyl alcohol. SDA 3C is 100 parts ethanol to 5 parts isopropyl alcohol. So when ordering denatured ethanol, be sure to specify either SDA 3A or 3C.

GLYCERIN

The term glycerin soap has come to be synonymous with transparent soap even though transparent soap can be produced without it. Nonetheless, most of the recipes in this book do include glycerin. Not only is glycerin an excellent solvent, but like castor oil, it acts as an emollient and humectant, drawing moisture from the air and holding it to the skin. *Used in excess however, the humectant properties of glycerin can cause a bar of soap to "sweat."*

Glycerin is actually an alcohol. Sweet and very viscous, it is a naturally occurring by-product of saponification. The reaction of a fatty acid and alkali create soap and glycerin, the percentage of glycerin being between 10-13%. In homemade soap production, glycerin is retained in the bar. Large soap manufacturers extract it and sell it as a valuable raw material. Synthetic glycerin, or propylene glycol, is derived from propylene, a by-product of petroleum distillation.

Glycerin can be found or ordered from drugstores and health food stores – scientific supply houses are another source. *Look in the Appendices for information.*

NOTE: When ordering glycerin and castor oil from scientific supply houses, ask for the "technical grade," which is less expensive.

Besides adding clarity to transparent soap, glycerin acts as an emollient and humectant – drawing moisture from the air and holding it to the skin.

SUGAR

The virtues of ordinary table sugar, or sucrose, in the making of transparent soap can't be overemphasized. Many formulations using only alcohol and glycerin for transparency often produce a slightly cloudy bar; a touch of sugar solution will render these same formulations perfectly transparent. Another virtue of sugar is its inexpensiveness. It can be used as a partial substitute for the spendier alcohol and glycerin.

Too much sugar in the soap, however, will cause stickiness and sweatiness – the same problem encountered with an excess of glycerin. And although sugar produces even greater transparency than glycerin, sugar lacks the humectant and emollient properties of glycerin.

Never substitute powdered sugar for granulated – it contains cornstarch which will ruin your soap's transparency.

ROSIN

Rosin, or resin, is the residue left after the volatile oils are distilled from the oleoresin of pine trees. Rosin comes in the form of transparent, pale yellow lumps. In soap formulations, it changes color and depending upon the percentage used, can create a deep root beer-colored bar.

Pure cane sugar is preferable to beet sugar for transparent soapmaking.

Rosin imparts a rich, creamy finish to a bar of soap and also prevents rancidity.

Rosin is not a crucial ingredient for transparent soapmaking, though it was quite popular with old-time transparent soapmakers. Besides its excellent transparency-producing properties, it imparts a rich creamy finish to the soap, has a wonderful fragrance and also prevents rancidity. *Too much rosin can soften and cloud the soap.*

STEARIC ACID

Stearic acid, or stearin, is a fatty acid derived from palm oil, tallow and other sources. Although some of the recipes in this book call for it, stearic acid isn't an essential ingredient for transparent soapmaking – but it does have some special uses. Being a free fatty acid, it's an easy way to adjust the soap's pH if the soap is too alkaline. It can be used as a substitute for palm and tallow. A small quantity of stearic acid added to an oil blend hastens saponification, cutting down on stirring time. It also makes a harder bar of soap.

Other fatty acids such as oleic can be used but stearic acid has a couple of advantages. It is relatively odorless (which isn't true of oleic and some of the other fatty acids) and is easier to find.

Stearic acid comes as a white, waxy flake. Scientific supply houses carry it. Also check with any local craft outlet which sells candle-making supplies, since stearic acid is often blended with paraffin wax to produce a slower-burning candle. *Other sources are listed in the Suppliers appendix.*

Stearic acid hastens saponification, makes a harder bar of soap and is relatively odorless.

PRESERVATIVES

Oils eventually turn rancid due to oxidation. The unsaturated soft oils are more easily oxidized than saturated oils such as coconut and palm. Transparent soaps seem much less prone to rancidity than opaque soaps. Perhaps this is due to the presence of alcohol, glycerin and sugar, which all have preservative properties.

Rosin acts as a preservative so the two rosin recipes in this book will need no additional preservatives. If you are concerned about rancidity in the other recipes, vitamin E is both natural and easily obtainable. Other natural preservatives are grapefruit seed extract and carrot root oil. For a twelve-pound batch of soap, two or three tablespoons of any of these oils should be sufficient. Add them along with color and fragrance right before pouring the soap into molds.

Natural preservatives are listed in the Suppliers appendix.

Transparent soaps are much less prone to rancidity than opaque soaps.

CHAPTER

EQUIPMENT AND PREPARATION

▶ BASIC EQUIPMENT

▶ MOLDS

▶ PREPARING THE LYE SOLUTION

Transparent soapmaking is fairly basic and can be done with equipment you already have in your kitchen.

Correct

measurements

spell the

difference

between success

and failure in

soapmaking.

T*he equipment necessary for transparent soapmaking is fairly basic. Most everything will probably be in your kitchen; if not, it can be borrowed from a friend or neighbor. If you pour soap regularly and want to eliminate some of the hand labor or if you desire more finished-looking wire-cut bars, Chapter 7 contains instructions and diagrams for building two inexpensive devices that are guaranteed to simplify your soapmaking.*

BASIC EQUIPMENT

Scales

Soapmaking is more akin to baking than cooking. Cooking can be improvisational and a good cook will often rely more on inspiration than written instruction. But correct measurements in baking and soapmaking spell the difference between success and failure.

Unless you can borrow one, an accurate scale will be your most expensive investment. All ingredients excepting color and fragrance need precise measurement. *The scale must be able to register increments as small as one ounce, and preferably able to weigh up to 20 pounds.* It might be worth your while to look around in second-hand shops and flea markets for used scales, but make sure you can test these out with an object of known weight. Or look under "Scales" in the yellow pages. A lot of these businesses carry used, reconditioned scales.

Mixing Pot

A two or three gallon pot (8-12 quarts) is an appropriate size for mixing the recipes in this book. If you want to double any recipes, a 4-gallon pot will be necessary. *Whichever size you choose, it must be either stainless steel or enamel, since lye corrodes most anything else.* Put lye in an aluminum pot and the pot fizzes and turns dull grey. *Enamel pots should be free of any rust. Rust in solution may cause cloudiness and mar the soap's overall transparency in the same way that mineralized water can.*

Thermometer

Your thermometer must be able to measure up to 160 degrees Fahrenheit. A candy or deep-fry thermometer with a stainless steel stem is best.

Stirrers and Mixers

For manual mixing, spatulas, stainless steel and wooden spoons work well. Whisks do the best job, particularly when stirring the alcohol into the soap. This dissolves the soap more completely; undissolved soap can mar the transparency.

Or try some of those miracles of the machine age. **Blenders and food processors are a fabulous way to thicken the oil-lye mix in a matter of minutes, though they don't work for every phase of transparent soapmaking.** You can also use an electric hand-held mixer, preferably secondhand so

Correct temperatures are critical for successful transparent soap. Make sure your thermometer is accurate.

as to avoid soaping up your favorite kitchen model. **Hand-held electric mixers not only eliminate manual labor, but the increased agitation thickens the soap solution more quickly.** *Take care to start on low speed to avoid splashing.*

Instructions and diagrams for constructing a very handy mixer out of an electric drill are given in Chapter 7. This mixer is useful for every phase of transparent soapmaking and will simplify the task considerably.

Goggles and Gloves

A must for mixing the lye solution and during the stirring of the soap. Use rubber bands for securing the tops of the gloves around your arms.

Containers

You'll need a few miscellaneous containers for your sugar solution, glycerin and alcohol. Quart-sized mayonnaise or cottage cheese containers work well.

Plastic Sheeting

Plastic sheeting will be needed for covering the soap pot after the addition of the alcohol. *Saranwrap and other kitchen films aren't heavy enough.* **Use heavy-duty plastic film, approximately two mls. thick –** this can be found in the painting supply section of your local hardware store. Clear plastic is best. The soap solution can then be watched as it mixes in the pot.

Plastic sheeting is also necessary for lining a wooden mold. *WARNING: Don't line wooden molds with used plastic.* Transparent soap is the viscosity of water when first poured, and like water it seeps out of the tiniest hole.

Bungee Cords or Flexible Rope

You'll use these to secure the plastic sheeting to the top of your mixing pot.

Cutters and Rulers

Any sharp kitchen knife will work for carving blocks of soap into bars. Or try using a square pastry blade or a stiff, 4-inch paint scraper; these two tools are pressed down into the soap to achieve a cleaner-looking cut. To create bars of uniform size, measure and score a grid on the top of the slab then cut.

A hardened slab of transparent soap will have a slightly uneven, pockmarked surface when first unmolded. This is created when small air bubbles present in the hot solution float up and imprint themselves on the cooling surface. A long-bladed knife or metal ruler works well for skimming this off. Another good scraping (and cutting) tool is a strip of sheet metal. You can get strips free by calling around to sheet metal shops – they usually have bins of odd-sized scraps which are otherwise bound for recycling. A piece two inches wide by approximately 16-18" long is ideal – being both flexible and easy to handle.

MOLDS

Transparent soap lends itself to a wide variety of molding possibilities. **Flexible materials such as plastic and rubber work best.** If the soap sticks to a less flexible mold, immerse the mold in hot water for a few seconds. This will slightly melt the soap away from the mold's surface. *Always make sure that the top of the mold is as wide or wider than the bottom and also be aware of any relief on the sides which could prevent the soap from releasing.*

Look around your house for mold ideas – tennis ball cans, plastic tofu trays, decorative plastic cookie box inserts, tart tins, milk cartons – there are many options. Plastic sheeting draped into a shoebox or cardboard box works fine. Or purchase a few plastic trays used for storing leftovers. Some are even divided up into bar-sized compartments. If you want fancy molds, pay a visit to your local craft or ceramic supply store – you should be able to find the ubiquitous seashells, scallops, etc. Kitchen accessory shops are another source. Metal molds, even aluminum, will not be a problem, since transparent soap is neutral when poured. *Whatever you end up using, just check for any holes!*

A simple wooden mold can be constructed in no time – you probably have enough scrap lumber in your garage or workshop to do the job. *See next page.*

Flexible materials such as plastic and rubber work best for molding soaps but there are many other possibilities.

Wooden Soap Mold

For a 12-pound batch of soap

1) Cut a piece of plywood or particleboard into a square measuring 14x14 inches.

2) For the sides use 1x3 or 1x4 inch boards. Cut two pieces 12 inches long and two pieces 13-1/2 inches long.

3) Then screw or nail them into the plywood and into each other where they abut.

4) Line the mold with plastic before pouring your soap, making sure the plastic drapes a few inches over the sides.

5) To eliminate most of the big creases in the plastic which will otherwise impress themselves into the hardened slab, first brush the bottom and sides of the mold with vegetable oil or a bit of glycerin. This will create a tacky surface to which the plastic will adhere.

6) Then lay the plastic in and smooth and flatten the creases.

The approximate yield for each recipe in this book is 11-12 pounds of soap. This will fill the wooden mold to a depth of approximately 2 inches.

SOAP MOLD CONSTRUCTION

SCREW OR NAIL TWO 1×4×12" BOARDS
AND TWO 1×4×13½" BOARDS TO A 14×14"
PIECE OF PLYWOOD.

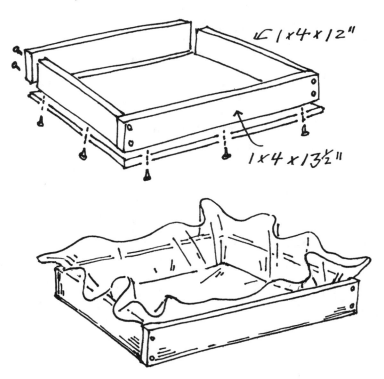

1×4×12"

1×4×13½"

BRUSH THE INSIDE OF THE MOLD
WITH VEGETABLE OIL OR GLYCERIN.
THIS WILL CREATE A TACKY SURFACE
TO WHICH THE PLASTIC WILL ADHERE.
SMOOTH AND FLATTEN THE CREASES.

PREPARING LYE SOLUTION

P**recise measurements are a must for the lye solution.** It's amazing what a difference it makes to your finished bar if the solution is a bit weak or a bit strong.

A half-gallon or one-gallon glass jar works well for mixing the water and soda beads. If the jar has a lid, pierce two small holes on opposite sides of the lid using an ice pick or screwdriver. The lye solution can then be added to the oil in a thin stream, ensuring more thorough mixing.

Enamel, stainless steel, glazed ceramic and plastic are also suitable for containing a hot lye solution. The plastic must be the heavier kind – the same thickness as a 5-gallon paint container or laundry detergent pail. *Never use aluminum, as explained earlier. Also make sure these containers have enough headroom for stirring.*

The procedure for making the lye solution is as follows:

- **With gloves and goggles on, measure the water and the soda beads separately. Use room-temperature distilled water.**

- **Mix them together, stir vigorously, *and avoid inhaling the fumes*.** The temperature of the water will rise to 200 degrees F. moments after the addition of the caustic soda. *Be careful – this steam contains lye.*

For successful transparent soapmaking, precise measurements are a must when preparing the lye solution.

Thorough stirring is important because unmixed caustic soda beads will quickly fuse together to form a solid white mass on the bottom of the container. This fused lye can be dissolved by setting its container (covered, to avoid inhalation of lye fumes) in a pan of boiling water. The heat will eventually dissolve this mass into the rest of the soda-water solution.

• **Mix your solution right before you measure and melt your oils.** By the time the oils have melted, the solution should be cooled down to the proper temperature- around 135-145 degrees F.

A finished bar of transparent soap can be ready for use within two weeks.

CHAPTER

MAKING TRANSPARENT SOAP

Getting

started . . .

Early transparent soaps were manufactured by dissolving flaked toilet soap in vats of boiling alcohol. The broth was kept boiling until the bulk of the alcohol evaporated out of solution; this alcohol was condensed and re-used in other batches. Dye and fragrance were stirred into the remaining broth which was then poured into molds for cooling. After the hardened blocks of transparent soap were removed from the molds and cut, the bars were placed into a warm, well-ventilated room for weeks, even months. One old recipe called for a drying time of one year!

Luckily, transparent soapmaking is much easier today. Finished bars of soap will be ready in two weeks. *The procedures and illustrations in this chapter will hopefully offer a clear and simple methodology for making you own transparent soap. (For an alternative to part of this procedure, see the "Alcohol/Lye Method" in the Appendices).*

FIRST MEASURE ALL INGREDIENTS

OIL BLEND (PALM OR TALLOW, COCONUT, CASTOR)

←LYE SOLUTION

PURE CANE SUGAR

SUGAR FOR SUGAR SOLUTION   GLYCERIN   ←ALCOHOL

THEN PROCEED TO STEP ONE ...

STEP ONE:
Mixing Oils and Lye

The lye solution and oils should be combined when they're both in a temperature range of 135-145 degrees F. This temperature is substantially higher than the range used for cold-process soaps; the higher temperature both accelerates saponification and helps ensure a more neutral pH. *Neutral soap is very important for the transparency of the finished product.*

STEP ONE: MIX OIL AND LYE, STIR SOAP UNTIL MIXTURE TRACES

TIME: FROM 3 MINUTES (WITH BLENDER) UP TO ONE HOUR (BY HAND)

TEMPERATURE: 135-145 °F

1) **Mix the soda beads and water right before you measure and heat the oils;** by the time the oils are warmed to 135-145 degrees, the lye solution should be just about the right temperature. *If it falls much below 135 degrees, set the container in a sink or pot filled with boiled water.*

STEP ONE CONTINUED . . .

2) **With your gloves and goggles on, begin adding the hot lye to the hot oils in a thin, slow stream.** Stir steadily and continuously.

3) **After pouring all the lye into the oil stir until the mixture thickens and "traces,"** *which means that when a small amount of the soap is scooped up and drizzled over the mixture's surface, it leaves a trace or trail before sinking back in.* Sometimes this is hard to detect unless the angle of light is just right. Tracing soap will be the consistency of a light gravy or sauce; it's color will also be whiter than when the lye and oil were first combined. *Tracing can happen in as little as three minutes (when using a blender), or take up to an hour (when stirring by hand). It depends upon the oils used and how quickly the mix is stirred.* Don't try to shortcut on time – you must stir the soap until it's traced – otherwise the soap will separate.

All soap,

whether opaque

or transparent,

must be stirred

until it traces.

Anything less

spells certain

failure.

If you are stirring the soap with anything besides a blender or food processor, check the temperature occasionally. If it drops much below 135 degrees before tracing, place over medium-low heat and gently bring the temperature back up.

The fastest and easiest way to trace soap is with a blender or food processor. The procedure is as follows:

• **By hand, stir the lye solution into the oils and mix for a minute to ensure a homogenous blend.** (You'll want to do this in another lye-proof container besides your soap pot, since the blenderized soap will be emptied into the soap pot.)

• **Then pour enough of this mixture into the blender to fill the blender half-way up.**

• **Mix the soap on low speed until it traces –** **it will be the consistency of a thin pudding.** This should take about 20-30 seconds.

• **Empty this into your soap pot,** then refill the blender with more oil-lye mix.

• **Repeat this process 6 or 7 times, or until all of the soap has run through the blender.** Then briefly hand-stir the pot of blenderized soap to ensure a homogenous mix.

Your whole

batch of soap

will trace in

a matter

of minutes.

If you construct a variable-speed drill mixer as outlined in Chapter 7, place the mixer over the pot, turn the mixer on medium and run the lye through the funnel. The mixture will trace more quickly than soap stirred by hand, but not as quickly as soap that's been run through a blender. Check the temperature occasionally. If it drops much below 135 degrees, gently warm on medium-low heat.

STEP TWO:
Covering the Soap: The Gel Phase

If you were making traditional opaque soap, color and fragrance would now be added to the tracing soap. The soap would then be poured into covered molds and allowed to harden.

For transparent soap:

1) **Place a lid over the pot and wrap the bottom, sides and top with a blanket or two.** The warmer the soap is kept, the more complete the saponification.

2) **Let the covered pot sit for an hour.** If you could watch the soap, you would first see it stiffen into the consistency of a very thick white paste. As saponification continues from the center of the pot outwards, this white mass bulges slightly then cracks to reveal a hot, amber-colored gel beneath. *This transparent gel is the colloidal state which all soap passes through before cooling.* Soon all of the

STEP TWO: COVER POT WITH LID THEN WRAP POT WITH TOWELS OR BLANKET. STIR MIXTURE ONCE.
TIME: 2-3 HOURS
TEMPERATURE: CHEMICAL REACTION WILL RAISE TEMP. TO 170-180°F.

soap is transparent and very hot – between 170 and 180 degrees Fahrenheit. Successful transparent soap in large part depends upon the soap passing through the gel phase – this is when the soap is neutralizing.

3) **At the end of one hour unwrap the soap. If it's still opaque and hasn't gelled, cover it back up until it does.** *The entire surface of the soap should be translucent, though there may be a thin white ring of cooler soap around the circumference of the pot.* **Stir the gelled soap for a minute, taking special care to scrape away the cooler, harder soap from the sides and bottom of the pot. Incorporate this into the hotter mass at the center of the pot.** At this point, any burns you might sustain won't be chemical, since the soap is neutralizing. Be more concerned about burns caused by the high temperature of the soap.

4) **After stirring, cover the soap for another hour.** Saponification is continuing, but eventually all the free alkalis and fatty acids will have reacted and saponification will slow. This slowing down is signalled by a gradual drop in the temperature of the soap. The soap is now near neutral. *If you want to test for neutrality, take a small sample and drop it into a glass of distilled water and stir. Neutral soap will easily dissolve. Another testing method involves the use of the chemical phenolphthalein. See the Appendices for its use.*

The time it takes for soap to gel is determined by 1) temperature of the soap, 2) how rapidly the soap has been stirred and 3) what kinds of oils you use.

Neutrality can

also be

tested using

phenolphthalein

(pronounced

fee-nol-thal-een).

This inexpensive

chemical takes

the guesswork

out of pH testing.

For instructions

on its use see

the Appendices.

GELLING THE SOAP
USING A DOUBLE BOILER

To hasten the gel time, create a double boiler. A five-gallon canning pot is ideal. Pour 3 or 4 inches of water into the pot and bring to a slow boil. Place a few spoons or knives on the bottom of the canning pot so that the soap pot has some water beneath it. Otherwise, the soap may scorch.

After the soap has traced, cover with a lid and place inside the canning pot. Keep the water at a gentle boil. Within 10 to 15 minutes the soap will begin saponifying; a ring of softer translucent soap will appear around the circumference of the pot. Stir the soap for a minute, taking care to scrape the bottom. Cover again. In the next 10 minutes, stir briefly 2 or 3 times. Air trapped in the soap mass may cause it to billow up, like a soufflé or rising bread dough. After 2 or 3 stirrings, the air should be gone. The soap will then need only an occasional brief mixing.

Neutralization should occur within 1 to 1-1/4 hours, but please test by dissolving a sample in water or by using phenolphthalein. You may then proceed with the addition of alcohol and glycerin.

STEP THREE:
Add Alcohol and Glycerin

You're now ready to dissolve the soap in alcohol and glycerin. But before that, please take time to read through the following section!

☞ Safety Procedures for the Use of Alcohol

It's very important to become familiar with the hazards of alcohol. This applies especially to anyone using gas heat. Alcohol must be kept away from open flames. It should pose no problem with electric ranges unless spilled directly onto an element.

Ethanol is very flammable. It's particularly problematic because when ignited, the flame is sometimes difficult to see. A few precautions and some common sense should safeguard any work area or kitchen against accidents.

1. **Equip the kitchen or work area with a fire extinguisher,** preferably an all-purpose 2A-10B:C. If you don't want to purchase or borrow an extinguisher, water will work. Alcohol is soluble in water, so what water actually does is dilute the burning alcohol. Apply the water as a spray, either out of a spray bottle or from the hose on your sink. Aim the spray at the base of the flames.

2. **Make sure the work area has adequate ventilation** – fans or open windows, and/or an exhaust vent over the range. You want to avoid a build-up of vapors; they may pose a fire hazard and cause dizziness if inhaled.

3. **Avoid the use of undersized pots for mixing soap.** Allow at least two inches of headroom after the addition of alcohol and glycerin to ensure against any spillage. Keep electric mixers on medium-low speed. Even after the addition of glycerin and sugar solution, a soap broth containing alcohol is still quite flammable.

4. **Store any unused alcohol in a break-proof container.**

SAFETY PROCEDURES CONTINUED . . .

These precautions are not intended to cause undue panic. Just as with the use of caustic soda, anyone exercising reasonable care with alcohol will have no problems. No soapmaking procedures involve pure, unmixed alcohol coming near a flame; *any problems will be encountered after it's been stirred into solution with the soap.* And since the alcohol is diluted in this form, it is substantially less flammable. Your soap pot will also be covered.

Only once in three years of transparent soapmaking have I experienced any trouble. While attending to another project, I absentmindedly left the soap heating on the gas range. It boiled over and the soap running down the sides ignited. Since there wasn't much actual spillage, the fire was easily contained. I was lucky.

If you do have a gas range and are nervous about fire hazards, use an electric hotplate. Just make sure it's in good condition and that it's *plugged directly into the wall and not into a small extension cord.* Otherwise, you'll just be creating further fire hazards.

Don't panic . . .

just exercise

reasonable care

when working

with alcohol and

you shouldn't

experience

any problems.

Now let's continue with Step Three – adding alcohol and glycerin . . .

1) **Uncover the pot and add the alcohol and glycerin.** The soap is probably still in the gel state and consequently quite warm. *So stand back a bit when adding the alcohol. Alcoholic vapors will be created as the alcohol is heated by the soap. These vapors are heady. At the same time,* the hot gel is being cooled by the solvents, and a portion of this gel now hardens into lumps of soap. Don't worry about these – they'll all eventually dissolve.

Now scrape all of the cooler, harder soap away from the bottom and sides of the pot using a spoon, spatula or your own hands – covered with rubber gloves of course. Scraping with your hands is most effective for this process since it allows you to feel any stubborn patches of sticking soap which might otherwise be missed by a spoon, particularly on the bottom of the pot. *Soap left on the bottom will burn when the soap is reheated. Sticking soap can also flake off right before the finished broth is poured; you'll then have transparent bars containing flecks of undissolved soap.*

STEP THREE: STIR IN ALCOHOL AND GLYCERIN, SCRAPE SOAP AWAY FROM SIDES AND BOTTOM OF POT, BREAK UP SOAP WITH WHISK.

STEP THREE CONTINUED . . .

☞ If you're using a variable-speed drill mixer the above procedure can't be done with the mixer. You must manually scrape the bottom and sides of the pot. Then the mixer can be placed over the pot and turned on. No plastic sheeting is necessary.

Whisks are the best utensil to use at this stage when stirring by hand. They help break up the soap mass so that it dissolves completely in the alcohol.

As soon as the sides and bottom are scraped and any large chunks broken up a bit with the whisk, that's enough. Your soap won't be completely dissolved at this point, but it will when the broth is heated.

2) **Now cut a double thickness of plastic sheeting, large enough so that several inches overhang the entire circumference of the pot.**

If you're stirring with a spoon or whisk, punch one small hole in the middle of the sheeting and run the stem of the utensil up through the hole. If you're using a hand-held electric mixer, punch two small holes for the stems of the rotor blades. Feed the stems up through the holes and lock them into the mixer.

3) **Secure the plastic tightly around the outer circumference of the pot with rope or bungee cord.**

NOW MAKE A "TENT" OF PLASTIC
OVER THE TOP OF THE POT,
SECURED BY ROPE OR BUNGEE
CORD. A HOLE IS PUNCHED
IN PLASTIC FOR A SPOON OR
WHISK; ALCOHOL-SOAP MIXTURE
IS STIRRED.

HANDLE OF WHISK
OR SPOON. TWO HOLES
CAN BE PUNCHED
IN PLASTIC FOR
STEMS OF
HAND-HELD
ELECTRIC
MIXER.

Pull gently up on the plastic so that the excess around the edges of the pot slides underneath the rope or cord and forms a slight "tent" three or four inches above the top of the pot. Trim off any excess plastic left on the sides since plastic is flammable. The tenting which you've created will give a little more ease and flexibility to the stirring you'll be doing for the next hour or so. If the plastic is taut, you'll only be able to stir small circles in the middle of the pot.

Are any alcohol vapors escaping through the gap between the plastic and the stirring handle? If so, attach the plastic to the handle with duct tape. If the tape doesn't hold, moisten a small cloth with water and wrap it over the opening. It might be a bit awkward, but it works. ***The importance of keeping the alcohol contained can't be overemphasized.*** The alcohol/soap solution will be heated and evaporating alcohol can spell cloudy soap.

4) **After making sure that there are no major vapor leaks in the plastic, put the pot on the stove. Turn the heat on medium and start**

Step Three continued . . .

stirring. If you're using an electric handmixer or the variable-speed drill jig, keep the speed on medium-low. This prevents both splashing and the formation of thick, billowy heads of foam. *A little air mixed into your solution is OK since the bubbles will eventually rise to the surface, but a thick head of foam can be difficult to subdue.* This often has to be skimmed off and tossed.

Stir for a couple minutes, then check the temperature of the solution by piercing the plastic with the stem of your thermometer. Turn off the heat when the solution reaches 160 degrees F. Continue stirring. By this time, any chunks of soap floating in the alcohol solution should be dissolving. *What you want is a clear amber liquid the consistency of water.*

9) **For the next 15-30 minutes, stir. Keep the temperature at 160 F.** The alcohol is dissolving the soap; the time this takes can vary. If the soap was hot and soft when the alcohol was added, 15 minutes should be enough time. If the soap was cooler and harder or if some of the alcohol is isopropyl (a less effective solvent than ethanol), it may take 20-30 minutes to completely dissolve. When in doubt, take a sample of the solution and hold it up to the light. Undissolved soap will appear as opaque specks floating in the clear solution. Stir until these disappear.

Correct temperatures are critical at this stage. Soap mixed at under 160 degrees may not dissolve completely.

STEP FOUR: ADD SUGAR SOLUTION
TO SOAP THEN TEST FOR
TRANSPARENCY.

— SPOONFUL OF SAMPLE WILL
HARDEN WITHIN FIVE MINUTES
AND INDICATE DEGREE OF
SOAP'S TRANSPARENCY.

← INVERTED DRINKING GLASS

STEP FOUR:
Add Sugar and Test for Transparency

1) **After the soap has completely dissolved, stop stirring.**

2) **In a separate pan, bring the water portion of the sugar solution to a boil then add the granulated sugar. Stir until completely dissolved.** Cover the pan and bring the sugar back up to a boil; let simmer for another 2-3 minutes. This will allow steam to wash off any undissolved sugar crystals adhering to the walls of the pot.

3) **Punch a small hole into the plastic tenting and insert a funnel. Pour the sugar solution into the broth and stir to incorporate.**

Now for the transparency test.

4) **Ladle out a spoonful of the solution and dribble it onto an inverted glass or bottle.** (To hasten the hardening time, chill the glass in the freezer a few minutes prior to testing the soap.) The degree of transparency found in this hardened sample will be mirrored by the transparency of the entire batch after it has hardened in the molds.

NOTE: Sometimes the top surface of the hardened sample may be somewhat milky. Rinse the sample briefly in hot water to dissolve this skin. If the rest of the sample remains milky, please consult the Troubleshooting chapter.

STEP FIVE:
Settling the Soap

When a spoonful

of your soap

mixture hardens

and remains

transparent it

will soon be

ready to pour

into the molds.

So whether your soap is right the first time or you've had to add a little extra of this or that, **when a spoonful hardens and remains transparent, the soap can soon be poured. But first you'll need to exercise just a bit more patience and cover the pot for another 20 minutes, or until the temperature of the soap drops to 140 degrees.**

During this time the soap is cooling and "settling." A cooler solution loses less alcohol to evaporation when the solution is poured into molds – cooler temperatures are also gentler on the fragrances. Settling the soap allows impurities in the broth to sink to the bottom and any air bubbles suspended in solution to rise to the surface. Foam caused by over-agitation will usually disappear during settling, but if it doesn't, skim it off. *Excess foam will harden along with the rest of the soap.*

STEP SIX:
Dyeing and Fragrancing

When the pot's uncovered this last time, the
solution will have cooled down a bit. There will
be a thin skin of hardening soap on the surface.
A few stirs is all it takes to dissolve this layer
back into solution. If it resists melting this
means that the soap stock is too cool, so put the
pot back on the stove, heat and stir for a minute
or two until everything's dissolved. This skin
won't ruin your soap but if it isn't stirred
back into solution it creates a blemish in the
finished bar.

Now the soap is ready for the addition of
the fragrance and dye unless you prefer
a neutral bar. Color and fragrance are added
to the liquid stock after it has settled for
15 or 20 minutes.

STEP SIX – ADD FRAGRANCE & DYE, POUR INTO MOLDS

☞ *Coloring and fragrancing ideas are*
presented in detail in the next chapter –
Chapter 5: Dyes and Fragrances.

STEP SEVEN:
Finishing and Cutting the Soap

Place the molds on a level surface where they can sit undisturbed for several hours. Lay some newspaper under them in case of spillage. Unless you're pouring into one large mold, you'll probably want to use a ladle or lipped measuring cup for filling smaller molds with the watery broth.

Before unmolding, make sure the soap is completely firm by pressing in the middle and feeling for any "give." Out of haste you might prematurely unmold the soap only to find that the inner core is still runny, like a chocolate with a liqueur filling. The soap then needs to be remelted and poured again. Once out of the molds, your soap will be transparent except for the top surface. This will appear a bit opaque and slightly pockmarked, due to tiny air bubbles which rose out of solution and impressed themselves here.

To give a finished look to the soap:

Take a knife blade or the edge of a ruler and gently scrape off the blemishes. Alter the direction of your swipes so that no gouges begin developing in one particular spot. **You can further polish the soap by rubbing with a soft cotton cloth or sponge dipped in alcohol, either ethanol or isopropyl.** The alcohol slightly dissolves the surface and gives the soap a more finished look.

As explained earlier, rapid cooling helps ensure transparency, so don't cover the molds or pour into molds that are excessively deep. Your soap will harden in 1 to 6 hours. The speed with which it hardens depends upon two things – the size of the mold and the formulation of the soap.

When cutting a large slab of soap into bars:

- **First measure off the desired bar sizes with a ruler or T-square.**

- **Gently score this gridmark into the top surface of the slab with a knife.**

- **After the slab is marked off, the bars can be cut with the knife or a pastry blade.** A stiff paint-scraping blade works well too. If these bars are too thick, turn them on their sides and cut to the desired thickness. *Whether or not you've poured into individual molds or into one large slab, the recipes in this book will yield between 40 to 50 average-sized bars.*

IF SOAP HAS BEEN POURED INTO ONE LARGE MOLD, CUT HARDENED SLAB INTO DESIRED BAR SIZE USING A RULER AND KNIFE.

When cutting and handling these bars, take care with fingerprints. The clear sticky surface of the uncured soap reveals all. Latex or thin surgical gloves are helpful for avoiding these blemishes.

STEP EIGHT:
Curing the Bars

Your bars need to be cured and hardened for two weeks. A warm, dry place is best, but don't get over-enthusiastic and set them in a warm oven or sunny window. If it's too warm, they'll melt.

SET BARS ON A RACK
OR TRAY AND CURE
FOR 2 WEEKS.

- Line the bars up on an empty storage shelf or plywood covered with wax paper. 18x18" plastic greenhouse trays work beautifully; the open grill-work on the bottoms allows for air circulation underneath the bars as well as around the sides and tops. Whatever you use, just make sure to leave a little space between each bar for air circulation.

During the curing time a skin forms on the bars. Water and alcohol begin evaporating out of the soap. Not only are your bars hardening, they're also becoming more transparent. This increased transparency is subtle but noticeable.

• At the end of two weeks, check your bars. Are they still a little soft? If so, give them another week. If you're impatient, go ahead and start scrubbing.

As water and alcohol evaporate from the curing bars, the bars become harder and more transparent.

ONE FINAL NOTE:

If for some reason you're dissatisfied with your finished batch of hardened soap – maybe you want a bit more color or fragrance or a different shaped bar – **the soap can be cut up and remelted over a double boiler.**

If you do remelt, it's best to do it within the first few days of the initial pour. Alcohol and water will be evaporating and you run the risk of reduced transparency if you wait too long. Even though older bars may be clear, the soap's structure is altered during a remelt and the soap can become cloudy or sticky.

HERE'S A QUICK RECAP OF CHAPTER 4:

1) MIX OIL AND LYE

2) COVER SOAP

3) DISSOLVE SOAP IN ALCOHOL & GLYCERIN

4) STIR ALCOHOL-SOAP BROTH

5) ADD SUGAR – TEST FOR TRANSPARENCY

6) FRAGRANCE & DYE

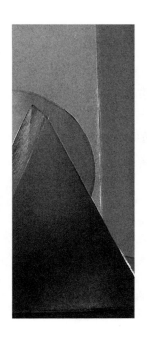

CHAPTER

5

DYES AND
FRAGRANCES

Fragrancing

and coloring

transparent soap

is a delight.

Transparent soap

can be dyed

with simple

food coloring

for beautiful

jewel-like bars.

All fragrances

remain

true and fresh.

*F*ragrancing and coloring transparent soap is a delight. Stir in the dyes and watch the soap change into a liquid jewel – ruby red, topaz yellow, emerald green. Food coloring is all you need. Transparent soap can be fragranced with either natural or artificial fragrances, but no matter what you use the fragrances remain true and fresh. The alcohol in the soap seems to act in the same manner as the alcohol base in a perfume – it "lifts" and intensifies the fragrances to such an extent that some are almost edible.

Uncolored, unscented soap is beautiful too. Your bars will be a shade of amber and have a light, clean smell. You might try dividing the batch up, pouring some plain soap directly into the molds then dyeing and fragrancing the rest.

Color and fragrance are added to the liquid soap stock after it has settled for 15 or 20 minutes. The solution is a bit cooler after settling, which is better for fragrancing since the volatile fragrance oils will be less prone to evaporation or alteration by the heat.

DYES

Food Coloring

If you've ever made opaque cold-process soaps and were frustrated by the skimpy palette of dyes available for coloring, you can unleash yourself with transparent soap.

Many dyes take a battering from the high initial pH of cold-process soaps and are often altered beyond recognition. So unless soap dyes are special-ordered, the color range for cold-process soaps is pretty much limited to earth tones. Transparent soap can be tinted in either subtle earth tones or bright primary colors, owing to its neutrality.

Ordinary food coloring found on the baking supply shelf of your local supermarket is all you really need. Each set of food coloring contains red, green, yellow and blue. The dyes come in either a liquid or a gel form. *If you purchase the gel variety, don't add the gel directly to your soap stock.* You can't control the color saturation as well since the clumps of dye will continue to dissolve over time. *Squeeze some of the dye into a glass or bowl and add a couple tablespoons of boiling water. Take a spoon or fork and stir until the clumps disappear.*

Schilling sells a set of liquid dyes which come in .25 ounce squeeze bottles. Whether you're using liquid or gel food coloring, one set of colors is enough to tint several batches of soap.

Transparent soap can be tinted in either subtle earth tones or bright primary colors.

Be conservative with the dye.
A little goes a long way.

Even though the soap is transparent, an over-saturation of color darkens the bar and consequently obscures the passage of light. The beautiful, gem-like quality of the transparency is then lost. To avoid this problem, start by adding just a few drops of dye to the stock. Pour some stock into a quart-size jar to a depth of one inch. This will help you judge how the color will look in a finished bar. If you want a deeper color add a few more drops to the stock and test again.

Blending dyes to make custom colors:

If you've ever taken a basic design class, you'll be familiar with the color wheel and the methods for blending two colors to produce a third. Red and yellow create orange, red and green make a shade of brown, red and blue yield purple, yellow and blue produce green. **Experiment a bit with mixing colors unless you're content with them the way they are**. *White cereal bowls work well for experimentation since the white background enables you to see just what your colors are without having to dab them on paper.*

Red, green and yellow food dyes used in tinting soap remain stable and true in color. *Blue is more problematic. It flattens and fades quickly – sometimes within a month or two. Exposure to* *direct sunlight hastens the fading.* You might try dyeing just a small portion of your stock with blue (or derivatives of blue such as purple) so that it can be used within a reasonable amount of time. The lack of a stable blue is the most lamentable shortcoming in food-grade dyes.

Besides the use of food coloring, you have several natural options.

Pears brand, the original transparent soap, is tinted with caramel coloring. Liquid chlorophyll comes in various shades of green from a mossy hue to a brighter grass green, and can be found in health food stores. Try ground turmeric, which yields a rich golden yellow, and ground paprika, which produces an orange-red. Cocoa powder, curry and cayenne pepper are other possibilities.

Don't add any of these powders directly to your broth. *Dissolve a few tablespoons of powder in a little water. Heat gently on the stove then pour through very fine cheesecloth or an old nylon stocking. Tiny flecks of unstrained spice will be visible in your soap if you don't take care with straining – unless speckles are the look you want.*

Create a more subtle and interesting palette of soap colors by combining two or more of the basic dyes.

Soap Dyes

There are limitations to food coloring. The lack of a stable blue is the most glaring, since it's a primary color. Consequently, other desirable blue-based colors like purple and turquoise will also be unstable and fade with time. Aside from blue, colors such as ruby-red and magenta are also impossible to blend using the basic food-color palette. If you're frustrated by these shortcomings, try soap dyes – they're available in a much broader spectrum of colors. *Sources are listed in the Suppliers section of the Appendices.*

NOTE: Don't use fabric dyes to color transparent soap. These dyes are stabilized with salt, and as mentioned earlier, mineral contamination can cloud the soap.

FRAGRANCES

Transparent soap is an excellent vehicle for fragrance. With opaque cold-process soap, the fragrance you smell in the bottle often flattens out or becomes almost unrecognizable in the finished bar. Fragrances maintain their integrity in transparent soap, staying full and round over time. The lower alkalinity of transparent soap is a big plus; it could also be that the solvents help maintain the fragrance's character. At any rate, you won't have to second-guess the fragrances for transparent soap. *What you smell is what you get.*

All fragrance notes, whether fruity, herbal-woodsy, spice, musks – remain true to the bottled fragrance. You might even add some of your favorite perfume.

Synthetic Fragrances

Some people have philosophical qualms about using synthetic fragrances. "They're not natural" or "they can cause allergies" are the most common objections. However, synthetic fragrances aren't completely synthetic – they are usually blended with some true essential oils. And true essential oils can cause allergies too.

There are many delicious artificial fragrances on the market now such as passionfruit, dewberry, and piña-colada; they make a perfect marriage with transparent soap. Most of these fruity notes go flat in a batch of cold-process soap; in transparents, you want to take a bite out of the bar. This is the reason why so many commercial transparent brands are so often fragranced with this particular family of scents. Other notes work just as well in transparents – musks, spices, herbal-woodsy. (*In the Appendices, you'll find a list of sources for these oils.*)

Most commercial soaps are scented at 1% – that is, for every one hundred ounces of soap stock, one ounce of fragrance is added. **The recipes in this book all yield approximately 11 to 12 pounds or about 170-190 ounces of soap; therefore you'll want to add about 2 ounces, or 4 tablespoons of fragrance.** This is also a matter of personal taste. *You may want to start with a bit less and try that out.*

One other advantage transparent soaps have over cold-process soaps: artificial fragrances don't cause the soap to thicken and "seize" in the pot before you have time to frantically pour it into the molds.

Most synthetic fragrances are a blend of some true essential oils **and** laboratory-produced scents.

If you've made cold-process soaps and have had this experience, you know just how horrible and hair-raising it is to watch all your expense and labor turn into an ugly lump in a matter of seconds. Cold-process soap contains a high percentage of unsaponified fatty acids and alkali before it's poured into molds.

The solvents in artificial fragrances produce a larger "interface" between the acids and alkali, dramatically accelerating saponification. You can relax and take your time with the transparent soap. The oils and lye have completely reacted by the time the fragrance is added; the solvents in these fragrances can even impart a little more transparency to the soap.

True Essential Oils

True essential oils are extracted from plant materials using steam distillation or mechanical expression. It's a marvel that the wood, leaves, flowers and fruits of plants can produce such a wonderful elixir.

There's much romance to essential oils. For instance, the history of rose oil: rose oil was mentioned in many ancient texts centuries before Christ, but this rose oil was probably not a true distillation from the flowers. Petals of roses were macerated, or soaked, in hot fats until the fragrance was infused into the fat. Legend has it that the first true rose oil was discovered by the wife of the Mogul emperor Jehangir in India.

The canals surrounding his palace gardens were filled with rose water, and one hot summer's day as his wife lazily drifted on the canals in her pleasure boat, she noticed an oily sheen floating on the surface of the water. She ordered that this oil be collected, and named the highly aromatic substance "Atr-i-Jehangiri."

Commercial perfumes are an orchestration of as many as 30 or 40 different oils in an alcohol base. *Oils of "high," "medium" and "low" notes are blended for an overall effect which changes with time,* just as a fine glass of wine produces many flavors and sensations after it's been swallowed.

High notes are created using more volatile oils with a high evaporation rate; citrus oils such as lemon, lime, orange, etc. are especially volatile. The high notes will be the first thing you smell in a perfume. They don't persist, however, and over time perfume changes character because the middle and low notes are emerging. These notes are composed of oils of lower volatility – that is, slower evaporation rates. **Musk, patchouli, oakmoss, vanilla resin, clary sage – all of these are lower notes and actually act as fixatives for the fragrances of both soaps and perfumes.**

You may want to create your own fragrances. There are books in print specific to perfuming; in fact, there's one which gives formulations for all the designer perfumes. Visit your local library.

If you do start experimenting, use an eyedropper and test everything in small quantities before committing yourself to larger quantities. Always write everything down.

If you experiment with creating your own scents, do everything in small quantities to start . . . and keep written notes for future reference.

Since transparent soap is very kind to fragrances you might not want to blend oils at all. Bars scented with a single oil, even the more unstable citrus oils such as orange, keep their fragrance for months. Added to cold-process opaque soap, essential oil of orange would be obliterated in a matter of weeks.

FRAGRANCE FORMULAS

Below is a variety of fragrance formulations using true essential oils.

Experiment first to find out just how a particular blend will smell. *Using an eyedropper, make one drop equivalent to one teaspoon. That way you won't use all of that expensive essential oil only to find out you really don't like the scent.* Squeeze a drop of the blend onto a sheet of paper and let it sit for a few minutes – the fragrance will change. Testing a few of these recipes by the dropperful will also give you a little more feel for perfuming.

WHITE LAVENDER:	TEASPOONS:
Lavender	6
Geranium	5
Clove	3

ELDERFLOWER:	**TEASPOONS:**
Bergamot	6 teaspoons
Thyme	3
Peppermint	3
Lavender	3

MILLEFLEUR:	**TEASPOONS:**
Orange	8
Cloves	2
Lavender	1
Nutmeg	3

ROSE:	**TEASPOONS:**
Rose or Geranium	3
Bergamot	5
Cedarwood	1
Sandalwood	3
Rosewood	2

BROWN WINDSOR:	**TEASPOONS:**
Nutmeg	4
Cassia	3
Caraway	2
Cloves	5

WHITE WINDSOR:	**TEASPOONS:**
Lavender	4
Thyme	2
Bergamot	4
Geranium	2
Cloves	2

If blending oils, put a drop of the blend onto a sheet of paper and let it sit for a few minutes. You will note a change in the fragrance.

ALMOND:	TEASPOONS:
Bitter Almond	7
Bergamot	7

LEMON:	TEASPOONS:
Lemon	7
Bergamot	3
Lemongrass	3
Cloves	1

SPANISH BOUQUET:	TEASPOONS:
Bergamot	4
Petitgrain	2
Orange	4
Lavender	1
Patchouli	1
Sandalwood	2

EARTH:	TEASPOONS:
Clary Sage	5
Thyme	2
Sandalwood	2
Bergamot	3
Clove	2

PATCHOULI:	TEASPOONS:
Patchouli	3
Cedarwood	2
Rosewood	4
Geranium	3
Sassafras	2

Wood, leaves, flowers and fruits of plants produce wonderful elixirs.

BAY LIME:	**TEASPOONS:**
Lime	6
Cedarwood	2
Petitgrain	1
Lavender	1
Anise	1
Cassia	2
Bay	1

NORTH WOODS:	**TEASPOONS:**
Spruce	3
Elemi	3
Cedarwood	1
Rosewood	3
Vetitvert	2
Bergamot	2

HONEY:	**TEASPOONS:**
Almond	2
Sassafras	1
Lemon	5
Vanilla	4
Clary Sage	2

EAU DE COLOGNE:	**TEASPOONS:**
Bergamot	4
Lemon	3
Lavender	2
Orange	3
Bay	1
Rosemary	1

Commercial perfumes are combinations of as many as 30 or 40 different essential oils in an alcohol base.

Use this page to

record your own

formulations or

to make notes.

All of the following recipes yield exceptionally transparent bars that vary somewhat in hardness, color and lather.

CHAPTER

6 Transparent Soap Recipes

The following recipes all yield very clear transparent soap. The kinds of oils used and the proportions of each in a given recipe will produce bars of slightly varying hardness, color and lather. Try a few different recipes and keep a couple of bars from each batch for comparison. Before proceeding, you might want to read the following section on substitutions.

Each fat and oil used to produce a bar of soap has its own unique chemistry which in turn affects the soap's hardness, solubility and lather.

SUBSTITUTIONS

- **Lard can be substituted for palm and tallow but produces a slightly softer bar of soap.** For some of the following recipes (such as recipes #2 and #6 which contain a high percentage of castor oil) the lard substitution might make the bars too soft. To compensate for this, subtract 3 or 4 ounces from the total weight of the lard and use stearic acid in place of the missing ounces. **Stearic acid will firm the soap.** *Melt the stearic acid separately and add after the other oils have traced. See recipe #4 for more details.*

- **Soft oils such as canola, cottonseed, olive, etc. can be substituted for castor oil, but remember that castor acts as a solvent as well as a saponifiable oil.** Therefore, soaps made with vegetable oils other than castor will not have as much transparency.

- **Isopropyl alcohol can partially substitute for the more expensive ethanol.** It is not as effective a solvent as ethanol; therefore, the transparency is inferior to soap made exclusively with ethanol. *Don't substitute all of the ethanol with isopropyl. Try a 25-35% substitution.* When purchasing the isopropyl at your local drugstore, be aware that different concentrations are sold – some contain more water than others. *A 99% solution is the one to buy.*

- **Palm kernel oil can be used in place of coconut, but not as much caustic soda is necessary for saponification.** If you wish to substitute palm kernel for coconut, please consult the Formulating section in the appendices.

 ONE MORE NOTE:

Do you want to reduce or increase a recipe?

Changes in quantities can sometimes adversely affect a formulation. The Formulating appendix contains information which can help you avoid problems.

THE RECIPES

These first three recipes are all very basic no-frills transparent soap formulations. Each recipe differs slightly in the proportions of the three basic oils – palm (or tallow), coconut and castor. All yield very transparent soap with rich, creamy lathers. You might want to make all three, setting aside bars from each batch for a comparison. This will familiarize you with the properties of the individual oils.

BASIC RECIPE #1

Lye Solution:

     12 ounces caustic soda

     1 pound 9 ounces distilled or soft water

Oil Blend:

     2 pounds 8 ounces palm oil, tallow or lard

     1 pound coconut oil

     1 pound 9 ounces castor oil

Solvents:

     1 pound 12 ounces ethanol

     8 ounces glycerin

Sugar Solution:

     15 ounces distilled or soft water

     1 pound 4 ounces sugar

BASIC RECIPE #2

Lye Solution:

    12 ounces caustic soda

    1 pound 9 ounces distilled or soft water

Oil Blend:

    1 pound 10 ounces palm oil, tallow or lard

    1 pound 11 ounces coconut oil

    1 pound 10 ounces castor oil

Solvents:

    1 pound 13 ounces ethanol

    15 ounces glycerin

Sugar Solution:

    13 ounces distilled or soft water

    1 pound 2 ounces sugar

BASIC RECIPE #3

Lye Solution:

    12 ounces caustic soda

    1 pound 9 ounces distilled or soft water

Oil Blend:

    2 pounds 8 ounces palm oil, tallow or lard

    1 pound 7 ounces coconut oil

    1 pound castor oil

Solvents:

    1 pound 14 ounces ethanol

    1 pound 4 ounces glycerin

Sugar Solution:

    13 ounces distilled or soft water

    1 pound 3 ounces sugar

RECIPE #4

Transparent Soap Without Palm Oil, Tallow or Lard

This recipe uses stearic acid as a substitute for the palm oil, tallow or lard. You'll want to mix the oils and the lye solution in a slightly different manner here. *Since stearic is a pure fatty acid it combines very rapidly with lye; within moments of pouring lye into an oil mix containing stearic acid the soap can thicken so quickly that stirring becomes impossible.* This thickening isn't the only problem. *The accelerated reaction can separate the lye and oil, curdling the soap.* No amount of subsequent mixing can reunite them.

What works with this recipe is to add the stearic acid last.

- Warm up the coconut and castor oils in the soap pot

- Then add the lye solution.

- Stir until the mass begins to trace. This will happen fairly quickly since the lye is in excess.

- Now add melted stearic acid. *(Mix this by hand if you're using the variable speed drill mixer – the stearic acid tends to clump and the mixer can't blend it uniformly in the pot).* It will quickly thicken the coconut/castor soap stock, but the stock won't separate. If the mass appears a bit lumpy, try to whisk the lumps out as best as possible – but don't worry overmuch, since these lumps will be thoroughly incorporated when you uncover the soap in another hour and whisk again.

Other than this one simple difference, the rest of the procedures for this recipe are the same as those outlined in Chapter 4.

Lye Solution:
    13 ounces caustic soda
    1 pound 11 ounces distilled or soft water
Oil Blend:
    1 pound stearic acid (melted and added
                                separately)
    2 pounds 8 ounces coconut oil
    1 pound 10 ounces castor oil
Solvent:
    1 pound 13 ounces ethanol
    1 pound glycerin
Sugar Solution:
    10 ounces distilled or soft water
    1 pound sugar

RECIPE #5

Copra Soap Transparent Bar

This is a recipe created exclusively for the transparent soap manufactured by Copra Soap. **The bar was designed to be mild, as transparent as other brands on the market, and firm enough to withstand the wear and tear of cross-country shipping.**

Like the recipe above, this recipe contains stearic acid, so follow the same procedure given on page 72 for adding stearic acid.

Lye Solution:
    11 ounces caustic soda
    1 pound 7 ounces distilled or soft water
Oil Blend:
    1 pound 9 ounces palm oil, tallow or lard
    1 pound 9 ounces coconut oil
    13 ounces castor oil
    8 ounces stearic acid (melted and added
                                separately)
Solvents:
    1 pound 13 ounces ethanol
    1 pound glycerin
Sugar Solution:
    12 ounces distilled or soft water
    1 pound 1 ounce sugar

RECIPE #6

Transparent Soap Without Glycerin

The term "glycerin soap" has come to be synonymous with transparent soap, but as will be seen with the following recipe, **glycerin isn't a crucial ingredient.**

Lye Solution:
>   12 ounces caustic soda
>   1 pound 9 ounces distilled or soft water

Oil Blend:
>   1 pound 10 ounces palm oil, tallow or lard
>   1 pound 10 ounces coconut oil
>   1 pound 10 ounces castor oil

Solvents:
>   2 pounds ethanol

Sugar Solution:
>   13 ounces distilled or soft water
>   1 pound 4 ounces sugar

TRANSPARENT SOAPS WITH ROSIN

Before proceeding with Recipe #7 and Recipe #8, a few paragraphs on rosin and its characteristics are necessary.

Rosin imparts wonderful qualities to transparent soap – a rich lather, an earthy aroma and color, and exceptional clarity.

An excess of rosin in a formulation, however, creates soft mushy bars, or bars which dramatically effloresce within a day or two of pouring. *Therefore stearic acid has been included in the following two rosin recipes to harden the soap and counteract this tendency.*

- **Rosin has a very high melting point and also becomes sticky when heated, so mix it with the stearic acid (which also has a high melting point) and melt together on medium-low heat.** Excessive temperatures will cause both the stearic acid and the rosin to darken.

- Stir occasionally to make sure the rosin dissolves. Since rosin is equally clear in both its solid and liquid states, unmelted pieces can go unnoticed.

- After the stearic/rosin mixture has melted, add it to the melted palm/coconut oil blend.

A bar of soap made with rosin will be rich in lather, exceptionally clear and have an earthy aroma.

Rosin has one more unexpected kink: when lye solution is added to a rosin/oil blend, the rosin causes the mix to rapidly thicken and curdle. Don't worry. Just proceed with the following steps:

- Whisk the lye into the rosin/oil blend as quickly and thoroughly as possible. The mass will appear quite lumpy.

- Cover the soap with blankets for 5-10 minutes.

- Uncover. The saponification rate is so accelerated by the rosin that the soap mass will already be gelling.

- Now the mixture will be a bit more manageable, so stir this for a minute or two. If the initial mixing wasn't enough to thoroughly homogenize the oil and lye, this second mixing should suffice.

- Now cover and let sit for the standard two hours.

Rosin is

distilled from

the oleoresin

of pine trees.

RECIPE #7
Deep Amber Rosin Bars

This recipe contains one pound of rosin – a lot of rosin. It imparts so much clarity to the soap that you'll notice a correspondingly smaller proportion of other solvents. The color of the finished bar is a rich nut-brown, the fragrance clean and earthy. *You won't want to add any extra color or fragrance.* The bar stands on its own. This is one of the author's very favorite recipes.

As mentioned before, rosin has a very high melting point and also becomes sticky when heated, so mix it with the stearic acid (which also has a high melting point) and melt separately. Make sure everything's dissolved before adding to the warm oil.

Lye Solution:
> 12 ounces caustic soda
> 1 pound 9 ounces distilled or soft water

Oil Blend:
> 2 pounds 2 ounces palm oil, tallow or lard
> 1 pound 5 ounces coconut oil
> 1 pound rosin
> 9 ounces stearic acid   } melt together in a separate pan – then add to above melted oils

Solvents:
> 2 pounds ethanol
> 14 ounces glycerin

Sugar Solution:
> 8 ounces distilled or soft water
> 8 ounces sugar

RECIPE #8

Jurassic Soap With Rosin

Another beautiful bar, though a lighter amber – the color of pine sap. With its color and trace of piney fragrance, you can almost picture a 200 million year-old insect embalmed within.

A great gift idea for kids: Drop a plastic insect into individual molds before pouring.

Lye Solution:
> 12 ounces caustic soda
> 1 pound 9 ounces distilled or soft water

Oil Blend:
> 2 pounds 2 ounces palm oil, tallow or lard
> 1 pound 8 ounces coconut oil
> 8 ounces castor oil
> 8 ounces rosin
> 6 ounces stearic acid } melt together in a separate pan – then add to above melted oils

Solvents:
> 2 pounds ethanol
> 12 ounces glycerin

Sugar Solution:
> 10 ounces distilled or soft water
> 1 pound sugar

Use this page to take notes on the recipes. i.e., how is the lather, color, hardness, etc.

CHAPTER

7

2 Easy-to-Make Tools,
or
**Taking a Little of
the "Hand" out
of Handmade Soap**

▶ MAKING AN ADJUSTABLE-WIRE BAR CUTTER

▶ MAKING A VARIABLE-SPEED DRILL MIXER

If you make soap

on a regular

basis or want to

eliminate some

of the labor

of stirring and

cutting, try

these tools!

If you're content with manually mixing your soap and hand-carving the bars, you don't need to bother with this chapter.

But if you make soap — either opaque or transparent — on a more regular basis and want to eliminate some of the labor of hand-stirring, and/or you want bars with crisp, wire-cut edges, read on . . .

Nothing could be more simple, economical and versatile than this homemade, adjustable-wire bar cutter.

Adjustable-Wire Bar Cutter

The light, portable cutter diagrammed here will cost very little for materials and take just a couple hours of your time to construct. It's designed to cut a 12x12x2" block of soap into any conceivable square or rectangular shape you wish to create. Professional soapmakers have more elaborate cutters with stationary wires, but for the home hobbyist, nothing could be more simple and versatile than this adjustable cutter. You can also take the basic concept and create your own.

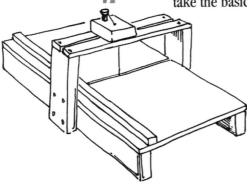

TO MAKE THE CUTTER YOU'LL NEED . . .

MATERIALS:

Amount	Dimensions of Lumber & Materials
2	2"x4"x28"
2	2"x4"x8"
2	2"x4"x3"
1	1"x2"x28"
2	1"x2"x20"
2	14"x17"x1/2" pieces plywood
2	14"x17" pieces formica or smooth linoleum (you should be able to find inexpensive scraps in the seconds bin of a flooring supply store)

HARDWARE:

- 1-1/2" and 2-1/2" wood screws
- contact cement
- one(1) 3/8" wide x 2" long hex-head carriage bolt
- medium-gauge guitar wire or 20 to 22-gauge music wire

TOOLS:

- drill
- utility knife
- hand or circular saw

PROCEDURE:

1) • **Contact cement the 2 sheets of formica or linoleum to the 2 pieces of plywood.**

   (Note: You don't need a special cutter for the

continued on next page . . .

Always wear

safety goggles

when working

with tools.

. . . continued from previous page

formica – a utility knife will do. Hold a ruler or T-square on the line you want to cut and gently but firmly score it several times with a utility knife. It will then snap along the line with gentle pressure.)

- **Allow the adhesive 15-20 minutes of setting time before proceeding to the next step.**

STEPS 1, 2 & 3

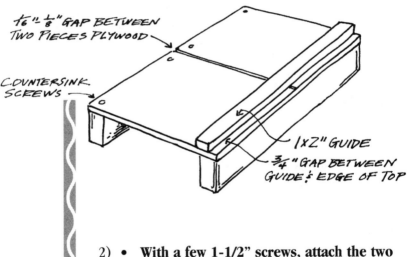

1/16" – 1/8" GAP BETWEEN TWO PIECES PLYWOOD

COUNTERSINK SCREWS

1x2" GUIDE

3/4" GAP BETWEEN GUIDE & EDGE OF TOP

2) • **With a few 1-1/2" screws, attach the two pieces of plywood (formica side up) to the two 28" 2x4's.** Leave a small gap between the two sheets – this will be the channel through which your adjustable cutting wire can slide. Countersink the screws so their heads aren't sticking up above the formica surface. Otherwise the heads can slightly gouge the soap as it's sliding across the top.

3) • **Using a few 1-1/2" screws, attach the strip of 1x2x28" wood to the formica top.** This is the guide edge for the block of soap as it's being pushed through. Leave a 3/4" margin between the guide and the edge of the formica.

Next – the carriage bolt.

STEP 4 - DRILL HOLE THROUGH HEX-HEAD BOLT

4) • **You'll need to drill a hole through the shaft of the bolt, about 1/2" down from the top. Mount the bolt in a vise and use a 1/8" or 3/32" drill bit;** it takes just a few minutes to bore through the shaft. If you know someone who has a drill press or works in a machine shop, you might have them do it.

This bolt will function exactly like a tuner on a guitar or piano. *Later, the cutting wire will be threaded through the hole in the bolt and the bolt will then be tightened into a wooden block.*

5) • **Take one of the 2x4x3" blocks and drill a 1/4" hole through the entire depth of the block.** This is the channel for the carriage bolt, but since it's a bit smaller than the bolt, you might need to tap the bolt with a hammer to get it started in the hole. *A snug fit is important*

continued on next page . . .

. . . continued from previous page

because pressure from the soap as it's pressed against the wire can unwind the bolt. The wire then loses its tension.

STEP 5

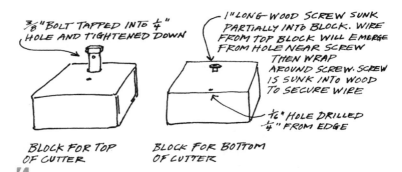

⅜" BOLT TAPPED INTO ¼" HOLE AND TIGHTENED DOWN

1" LONG WOOD SCREW SUNK PARTIALLY INTO BLOCK. WIRE FROM TOP BLOCK WILL EMERGE FROM HOLE NEAR SCREW THEN WRAP AROUND SCREW. SCREW IS SUNK INTO WOOD TO SECURE WIRE

1/16" HOLE DRILLED ¼" FROM EDGE

BLOCK FOR TOP OF CUTTER

BLOCK FOR BOTTOM OF CUTTER

- **Using a crescent or socket wrench tighten the bolt 1" into the wood.**

- **With a smaller bit – 1/16" or so – drill another hole completely through the block 1/2" distance from the bolt.**

- **Now take the other 3" block of 2x4" and drill a 1/16" hole through that too, about 1/4" from the edge of the block. Partially sink a 1" wood screw into the middle of the block.**

6) • **Screw or nail the two 2x4x8" blocks onto the sides of the cutter.** *Make certain the middle of each block is aligned with the groove between the two sheets of plywood.*

7) • **To the tops of these 2x4x8" blocks, screw down the two 2x2x20" boards side by side, leaving a slight gap between them.** *This gap should line up with the groove between the sheets of plywood below.*

It's now time to string your cutter . . .

A medium-gauge guitar wire works well – you want to avoid a wire that's too fine, as it might snap as the soap is being pushed through. An overly-thick wire will offer too much resistance to the soap. Buy one or two extra back-up wires in case of breakage. Or you can get what's called music wire. This comes in a quarter or half-pound roll and is much more economical than guitar wire.

continued on next page . . .

STEPS 6, 7 & 8

GAP BETWEEN 1X2X20" BOARDS ALIGNED DIRECTLY OVER GAP BETWEEN PLYWOOD SHEETS

WIRE ATTACHED TO BOLT THEN FED THROUGH BLOCK AND DOWN TO BLOCK UNDERNEATH FRAME. TIGHTEN BOLT TO TIGHTEN WIRE

2X4X8"

... continued from previous page

It's also more difficult to find. Try calling a piano tuner or rebuilder in your town — they might special order it or sell you some of their own. If not, contact the suppliers listed in the Appendices. *A 20 or 22-gauge music wire is ideal for cutting.*

8) • **Thread the guitar wire or a 2-foot length of music wire through the hole in the carriage bolt.** (The carriage bolt should be tightened into the 3" block).

• **Loop the end of the music wire once around the bolt and tie a knot.** You might have to use pliers to do this. *Clip off excess wire. If you're using guitar wire run the length of the wire through the bolt until the metallic knob at the wire's other end hits the bolt. The knob is enough to secure the guitar wire — you don't need any knots.*

• **Feed the free end of the wire through the 1/16" hole next to the bolt.**

• **Now set this block of wood on top of the two 1x2's which form the "bridge" across the cutter.**

• **Pass the wire through the gap in the bridge, then on down into the narrow channel running the width of the formica top.** *Your wire should now be sticking out through the bottom of the cutter.*

- **Flip the cutter over. Thread the wire through the other 3" block, starting on the side without the wood screw.**

- **Pull the wire taut then wind it a few times around the screw head and tie a knot.**

- **Sink the rest of the screw into the wood.** This will secure the wire to the bottom block. Clip off excess wire.

Now, flip your cutter right-side up.

- **Tighten the wire. This is done by turning the carriage bolt with a socket or crescent wrench.** *(Make sure you twist clock-wise so the bolt is sinking deeper into the wood. You don't want to be tightening the wire at the same time you're unscrewing the bolt from the block).* The hex-head bolt functions in the same manner as a tuner on a stringed instrument. **Don't tighten too much – wire with too much tension tends to snap under the pressure of the soap.** Tight, but not too tight. The tightened wire should hold the 3" block of wood underneath the cutter snug against the plywood.

Your cutter is done!

continued on next page . . .

. . . continued from previous page

TO USE YOUR CUTTER . . .

Before cutting, fill a spray bottle with water or isopropyl and lightly moisten the cutter's surface – this makes for easy, frictionless pushing. The smooth linoleum or formica top won't mar the surfaces of your soap, plus it's easy to clean. You'll also need to make the cutter somewhat stationary so that it doesn't move while you're cutting soap. This can be as easy as abutting it against the wall behind your kitchen counter top or clamping it to a table.

By sliding both the top and bottom blocks, the wire will move back and forth to create any size bar you desire. *If you find the wire doesn't go all the way over to the wooden guide, flip the cutter over. The moveable wooden block underneath the cutter probably needs to be rotated.*

As you push your block of soap through the cutter, try to push in towards the guide board as well as forward. *In other words, concentrate on pushing in an imaginary diagonal direction. The block of soap can wobble if it's not pushed into the guide and you'll end up with wavy edges to your soap.* Try using a small length of 1x2" wood to push the block of soap. It gives you more control, plus alleviates dent marks and fingerprints.

If you constructed the wooden mold diagrammed in Chapter 3, one recipe will yield a 12x12x2" slab of soap. **Before cutting bars, "clean" the slab. Set the wire about an 1/8" from the guide and gently push the block through. Trim all four sides. Then gently scrape off the flaws on the top and bottom of the block. These trim scraps can be remelted or used as-is.**

Now the block is ready to be cut into bars. If you want a 2x3x1" bar of soap:

- **First take a ruler and measure 2 inches over from the wooden guide.** Jiggle your wire over to this spot and tighten if it's a bit slack. *Also eye it to make sure the wire is straight up and down, not at an angle.*

- **Push the trimmed slab through until you're left with 6 two-inch wide strips.**

- **Now measure over 3 inches from the guide and move the wire here.**

- **Run the strips through sideways and cut into 3" lengths.** You now have blocks of soap measuring 2x3x2" deep. For a 1" thick bar of soap, set your wire one inch from the guide, flip your bars on their side and push them through again.

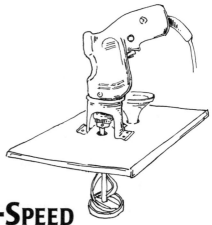

VARIABLE-SPEED DRILL MIXER

This mixer may look a bit primitive but it works like a dream. If you own a variable-speed drill, it costs next to nothing. There will be no plastic tenting to bother with and no manual stirring.

TO MAKE THE MIXER YOU'LL NEED . . .

MATERIALS:

- One square of plywood, sized to cover the entire top of your soap pot. Add an extra inch or two for a little overhang

- One tin can, 3" in diameter, 4" high (dog or catfood can size)

- 6 half-inch wood screws

- One 5-gallon paint mixer for 3/8" electric drills, found in most any hardware or paint supply store

- One variable-speed 3/8" drill with set button

TOOLS:

- **Hand or circular saw, drill, tin snips, pliers, hacksaw**

PROCEDURE:

1) • **Cut the plywood to fit over the top of your mixing pot; add an inch or two to compensate for any movement of the board during mixing.** If your pot is 12" in diameter, cut the plywood in a 14x14" square. If you have a jigsaw, cut a circle 14" in diameter.

2) • **Eye or measure the center point of your board and drill a 1/2" hole.** This hole is for the shaft of the paint stirrer.

- **4 or 5 inches out from the center hole drill a 3/4" hole.** The neck of a small funnel will fit in here.

- **Drill a third hole 1/4" in diameter 3 or 4 inches out from the center in any direction.** This is for the shaft of your thermometer.

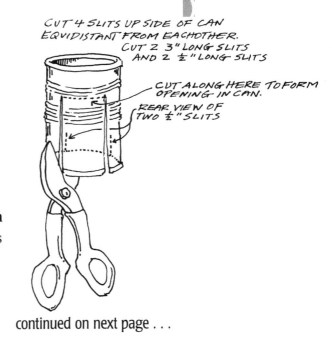

CUT 4 SLITS UP SIDE OF CAN
EQUIDISTANT FROM EACHOTHER.
CUT 2 3" LONG SLITS
AND 2 ½" LONG SLITS

CUT ALONG HERE TO FORM
OPENING IN CAN.
REAR VIEW OF
TWO ½" SLITS

continued on next page . . .

... continued from previous page

3) • **Remove the top and bottom of your tin can.**

• **With tin snips, make four 1/2" cuts equidistant from each other up the side of the can (at 12, 3, 6, and 9:00 respectively).**

• **Select any two adjacent cuts and continue snipping to within an inch from the top.**

• **Snip off the flap formed by these two long cuts. With pliers bend all of the sharp edges in.** *This will keep any fingers from being cut.*

• **Use pliers to gently fold out the remaining three 1/2"-long flaps of metal.**

• **Tap two holes into each of the three flaps with a hammer and nail.**

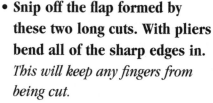

WITH PLIERS, GENTLY BEND BOTTOM OF CAN OUTWARD TO FORM 3 ½" LONG METAL FLAPS. PUNCH TWO SMALL HOLES IN EACH FLAP. SLIGHTLY BEND BACK SHARP EDGES AROUND THE OPENING.

4) • **Set the tin can over the 1/2" center hole in the plywood.** The middle of the can should sit dead center over the hole.

• **Attach the can to the board by sinking 1/2" screws into the wood through the holes in the flaps.**

5) • **With the hacksaw, cut the mixing blade to size.** The paint mixers come with 17" shafts, which is much too long for any mixing pot. You'll want to saw it so that the blade clears the bottom of your pot by at least a 1/2 inch.

PAINT MIXER FOR ⅜" DRILL

An easy way to do this is . . .

• **First measure the height of your pot.**

• **To this number add another inch and a half. This will be the approximate length you'll need to cut the mixer blade, as measured from the tip of the stirring end.** For instance – if your pot is 7" high, you'll need to saw the mixing blade to 8-1/2". You may need to adjust the blade length with another small cut to get it to fit just right.

☞ **One precaution about the paint mixers. They usually come coated with a colored varnish. You might want to take some paint remover and strip this away before you make soap, otherwise over time the lye from your soap dissolves the varnish. This varnish is a bit toxic, but since it takes many mixings to completely dissolve the coating it probably isn't cause for much concern. The varnish will also faintly tint your finished soap.**

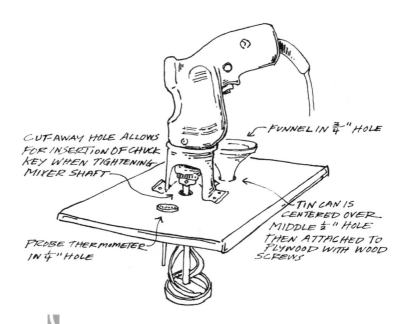

CUT-AWAY HOLE ALLOWS FOR INSERTION OF CHUCK KEY WHEN TIGHTENING MIXER SHAFT

FUNNEL IN ¾" HOLE

TIN CAN IS CENTERED OVER MIDDLE ½" HOLE THEN ATTACHED TO PLYWOOD WITH WOOD SCREWS

PROBE THERMOMETER IN ¼" HOLE

To use your mixer . . .

1) **Stick the mixer shaft up through the plywood's center hole then lower the tip of the drill into the can.** The cut-away hole on the side of the can enables you to stick the chuck key through and tighten the chuck around the mixing shaft.

2) **Before lowering the drill into the liquid adjust its speed.**

   - For the blending of the oil and lye run the mixer on medium or higher, but not so high as to cause the soap to splash to the top of the pot.

   - For the alcohol/soap stirring, turn the speed to medium-low; this prevents the formation of foam which can be difficult to subdue.

3) • **The funnel allows you to add ingredients such as lye and sugar solutions with minimal fuss.** *Take care to stuff a small wad of plastic wrap into the funnel neck after the addition of the alcohol – this will help contain the vapors.*

4) • **The thermometer rests permanently in its slot so that the temperature can be constantly monitored. There's no need to manually dip the probe every few minutes as with hand mixing.** *If the shaft of the thermometer isn't totally immersed in the liquid, the temperature reading on the dial may register a slightly lower than actual temperature.*

• **To correct for temperature discrepancies, first dip (by hand) the thermometer shaft into the soap stock.** Let's say it reads 160 degrees F.

• **Next slip the thermometer into its slot on the mixer frame.** Set the mixer over the soap pot and take this temperature. Say it reads 150 degrees. You now know there's a discrepancy of 10 degrees, so in the future you'll heat the stock accordingly, without having to hand-dip for an accurate temperature.

The mixer is useful for every stage of transparent

continued on next page . . .

. . . concluded from previous page

soap production with one exception: *You must hand-stir the alcohol into the soap and manually scrape the the soap off the sides and bottom of the pot.* **After the pot's surfaces are clean turn the mixer back on and proceed.**

With this mixer, the only thing necessary to adjust is the stove heat. If you find the tin can set-up a bit too primitive, you can purchase drill guides at hardware stores although they are quite expensive.

NOTE: The gap between the center hole and the mixer shaft will allow the evaporation of a small amount of alcohol. It shouldn't be cause for much concern, but if you want to seal the gap, create a gasket with a piece of rubber. Cut a small hole in the middle of a 3 x 3" square of thin rubber (an old inner tube will do) and staple the rubber to the underside of the plywood, aligning the hole in the rubber with the center hole of the plywood.

CHAPTER

8 TROUBLESHOOTING GUIDE

Failure in making soap is almost always a result of improper measurement of ingredients or temperature.

Failure in making soap – either opaque or transparent – is almost always a result of either improper measurement of ingredients and/or temperature, or undermixing. Take care that your scales and thermometers are accurate and that will alleviate 98% of possible problems. One of the beauties of transparent soapmaking is that some problems can be rectified when the soap is in the alcohol solution phase, but that's no license to abandon care and precision. Sometimes no amount of tinkering can right the wrong, and you're stuck with a cloudy batch of soap.

The following list delineates most of the problems you'll encounter and offers some possible solutions:

Problem:

1) SOAP MIXTURE DOESN'T THICKEN AND TRACE

Solution:
None of the recipes in this book should take much over an hour to trace with manual stirring, so if you're still stirring after two hours, read on.

Most likely the problem is either too little lye or too much water.

Though there is no way at this point to be absolutely certain of which one, chances are it's the lye because unless water was added in substantial excess, the soap is generally forgiving of a little extra. Try adding a bit more lye solution. Start with an ounce of dry caustic soda and mix with two ounces of water. Cool it down for a minute or so then add to the soap stock.

Mix for another ten to fifteen minutes and look for signs of tracing. If nothing has happened, add three more ounces of lye solution. Stir some more. Unless your initial measurement of caustic soda was terribly off, the soap should trace after two or three of these smaller additions.

A soap stock that's too cool will take a longer time to trace. If your thermometer is accurate, check this possibility off.

Undermixing is another culprit, particularly if you stir by hand.

The faster the lye and oil are brought into contact, the quicker they saponify and trace. This is one advantage of electrical mixing over manual. If you don't have a blender or food processor, borrow one now and mix.

If none of the above techniques work for your stubborn soap, it's wisest to start again. You might want to pour the discarded mix into a plastic-lined mold and cover for 24 hours just to see what happens. It could end up hardening into respectable opaque soap.

Problem:

2) SOAP CURDLES AND SEPARATES

Solution:

> **Mismeasurement of ingredients and/or wide variations between the temperatures of the lye and oils usually cause this problem. Slow, uneven stirring can also contribute, so try mixing curdled soap in a blender or food processor.**

If the batch still remains curdled after blending, it's best to toss it out because the problem is probably due to an excess of lye.

Rosin and stearic acid in an oil mix will curdle even if everything is measured correctly, so don't panic. Just follow directions for their use in Chapter 6.

Problem:

3) SOAP DOESN'T GEL

Solution:

If your soap traces (i.e. – you've measured all the ingredients properly) and its temperature is around 135-145 degrees before covering the pot, there should be no problem with gelling.

> **Failure to reach the colloidal state will either be due to insufficient or excessive lye, too much water in the stock or a low temperature.**

Nothing can correct an excess of lye.

An excess of lye is usually noticeable in the appearance of the soap after it's rested under the blankets for a while. Good soap will turn hard and pasty before gelling, but if the soap stays pasty and doesn't pass into the gel state, or gels only slightly before firming up again, there's too much lye. Throw it all out.

Deficiency of lye can possibly be corrected by following the instructions given in Section One above for "Soap That Doesn't Thicken or Trace," providing your soap at this point isn't too thick to stir.

A too-low temperature is the easiest problem to correct. Place the pot over a double boiler and heat. Use the double-boiler method described on page 38.

Problem:
4) SOAP DOESN'T DISSOLVE IN ALCOHOL

Solution:

The temperature of your alcohol/soap stock needs to be in the 150-160 degree range to dissolve the soap completely. Make sure your thermometer is registering correctly. If the soap has difficulty dissolving after you've stirred it for several minutes at the proper temperature or if the stock is somewhat thick and viscous, you haven't measured your alcohol correctly.

continued on next page . . .

. . . continued from previous page

To correct, add two ounces of alcohol at a time and stir. Keep adding in small increments until all the soap dissolves or any syrupy thickness to the broth is thinned to the viscosity of water.

NOTE: Soap dissolved in an ethanol/isopropyl blend will take longer to dissolve.

Problem:

5) CLOUDY SOAP

Solution:

After you've added the sugar solution, then poured a small test sample only to find the sample clouds upon hardening, don't worry too much. It's almost always fixable unless your initial measurements of lye and oils were way off.

> **Usually four or five extra ounces of solvent will dissipate the cloudiness.**

If four or five extra ounces of sugar solution, alcohol or glycerin don't solve the problem, you'll have to tinker a bit more. Just remember to keep the heat near 160 degrees and be sure to do all your adjustments while the soap's still in the pot, using small tests on glass as your indicators. The transparency of these samples will be identical to the finished bars of soap. If there's some cloudiness in the test samples it won't work to cross your fingers and pour the soap into molds, hoping for the best. *Before taking corrective measures please continue reading this section.*

Cloudiness can be caused by:

a) **Not enough solvent.** An insufficient amount of either alcohol, glycerin and/or sugar solution is the most likely reason for cloudiness providing your measurements of lye, oils and temperature were correct. Transparent soap needs a certain amount of these solvents for perfect clarity; even a shortage of water in the lye or sugar solution can impair transparency.

This problem is the easiest fix. Use the sugar solution to adjust with first because sugar solution produces the best clarity. And it's cheapest.

If your first test sample on glass turns milky, add 3 ounces sugar solution to the liquid stock and stir for a half minute to incorporate. Pour another small sample onto glass. If it's still milky, add another 3 ounces and stir again. Don't repeat this procedure more than two times since excess sugar in the soap can cause softness, sweating or even cloudiness in the hardened bars. Instead, try a few ounces of alcohol. Soap that's still milky after 8 to 10 additional ounces of solvents will probably be suffering from some other problem, such as mismeasurement of ingredients. If you want to continue adding solvents, be forewarned – too much solvent will prohibit the firming up of the soap after it's poured into molds or produce soft, sticky bars.

continued on next page . . .

. . . continued from previous page

b) An excess of solvents. Cloudiness can be caused by an excess of solvents as well as by a deficiency of solvents. Perfectly transparent soap seems to exist in a somewhat narrow window, balanced between too little and too much solvent.

A deficiency of solvents usually gives the soap a uniform hazy appearance. An excess often manifests as soft, sticky soap, or soap that doesn't firm up very well. Mottled, blotchy areas surrounded by areas of clear, firm transparent soap is another sign of excess solvents. These blotches are milky and soft and are often more pronounced near the center of a large slab, the reason being that the soap has taken longer to cool here. Slower cooling times promote cloudiness, and excess solvents delay the cooling and hardening of the soap even further.

Overaddition of either glycerin or sugar solution will be the likely cause. As mentioned in the chapter on ingredients, both of these solvents can cause stickiness or cloudiness when used in excess. An excess of alcohol will not produce this problem. Rosin-based soaps are particularly sensitive to excess sugar. Two or three extra ounces of sugar in one of these formulations can cause cloudy areas that grow almost like a bread mold. What begins as a few random white patches spread and engulf a large slab of soap within 3 or 4 days, turning the slab into white pasty mush.

If you think your soft or mottled soap is caused by an excess of solvents, try remelting the soap. Then pour it into smaller molds and flash-cool it in the freezer or refrigerator to render it transparent. This doesn't always work. The best antidote for mushy soap is to first remelt it, then add melted stearic acid and lye solution. In essence, you're adding more soap to the soap. Stearic acid works much more effectively than extra palm or coconut oils. Stearic not only produces a harder soap that consequently cools more quickly (thus retarding the formation of crystals), but it also saponifies much more rapidly than an oil, requiring less mixing time.

For every ounce of stearic acid added to the remelted soap, add a half an ounce of standard lye solution. The amount of extra stearic acid/lye solution necessary will depend upon how blotchy the soap is. There aren't any hard and fast rules. If the slab appears only slightly blotched, you might start with 3 or 4 ounces of melted stearic acid. For badly mottled soap, try 7 or 8 ounces. Add to the 160 degree soap stock, stir for 10 to 15 minutes, settle, then repour into the molds. Unfortunately, you can't dribble a test sample on glass and get an accurate reading as to the transparency of the whole batch. This seems to be the one exception to that principle. A small sample cools quickly enough to prevent the formation of soft spots which will manifest in a larger, more slowly-cooling mold. So pour and wait. If you have to remelt a second time, add 3 or 4 ounces of alcohol along with the additional stearic acid/lye to compensate for any evaporation.

continued on next page . . .

. . . continued from previous page

c) **Too much lye, too little lye.** This is where phenolphthalein really comes in handy. When dropped onto a sample of soap it allows you to assess the situation immediately. For instructions on using phenolphthalein, go to the Appendices in the back of the book.

Old-time transparent soapmakers didn't have phenolphthalein and relied instead upon squeezing the hardened sample with their fingers. Here is their simple method: Press your finger into the milky sample. If it splinters into numerous small sharp-edged pieces, the lye is in excess. A milky sample that feels soft and greasy and flattens out under pressure is a sign of too little lye.

If the test indicates an excess of lye, proceed with this technique: Melt a few ounces of stearic acid. Add two tablespoons to the stock and stir for 15-20 minutes. Keep the temperature at 160 degrees. Saponification is resuming and time is needed for neutralization of the stearic acid and lye. After 20 minutes, scoop out a sample and test again. If the sample is still milky, repeat the process. Continue adding stearic acid until the mixture tests clear.

If the soap-squeezing test indicates too little lye, mix up some extra lye solution. This doesn't have to be accurately weighed. Pour a quarter cup of dry caustic soda into half a cup of distilled water and stir. Add two tablespoons of this solution to the soap stock and mix, using the exact procedure outlined in the paragraph above for soap containing an excess of lye.

d) **Incomplete Saponification.** There's a good chance cloudiness will result if you don't allow the soap enough time in the gel state. This is a crucial phase when the fatty acids and lye are reacting and neutralizing. If your soap takes longer than an hour to gel, wait until it does. Then stir and cover for an hour. Another option is to use the double-boiler method outlined on page 38. However, if it hasn't gelled after three hours something is wrong – probably your measurements of oil and/or lye.

e) **Over-evaporation of alcohol.** If you let the alcohol/soap stock's temperature rise much above 160-170 degrees for extended periods of time, or if your pot isn't well-covered, alcohol will evaporate quickly. Some evaporation during mixing is inevitable, but beyond a certain point enough is lost to cause cloudiness in the finished bar. It's a difficult problem to diagnose. One trick that works (providing that you are absolutely certain you measured everything correctly) is to add up all of the weights in the written recipe, then weigh your cloudy stock. Compare the two numbers. If the weight of the stock is substantially lower than the recipe's weight, add more alcohol. NOTE: You won't have to make up the entire difference with alcohol. A portion of the difference will be enough to restore clarity, so add incrementally. Stir for a minute or so after each addition, enough to ensure thorough incorporation into the stock. Sample on glass each time.

continued on next page . . .

. . . continued from previous page

f) **Contamination.**

1. Undissolved soap. Make sure that the soap/alcohol stock is heated to 160 and stirred long enough to dissolve the soap. Undissolved soap appears as opaque, odd-sized bits surrounded by clearer soap. Try remelting and stirring for another 15 minutes.

2. Undissolved sugar. In the beginning of this book I likened soapmaking to baking. In truth, candymaking is a better analogy. All three arts require accurate measurement of weights and temperature, but soapmaking and candymaking in particular revolve around the avoidance of one main problem – unwanted crystallization.

   Undissolved sugar is a contaminant which can trigger the formation of crystals. These will eventually multiply and revert the transparent soap back to its opaque state. Small white areas usually appear within a day or two after pouring and quickly spread. Care must be taken when preparing the sugar solution – don't shortcut on the procedure outlined on page 45.

3. Mineral contamination. A clean, rust-free soap pot and the use of distilled or soft water are very basic ways to avoid 99% of all mineral contamination.

   On the bottom of the list of suspects causing cloudy or crystallizing soap is the possibility of contaminated raw materials. Alcohol, caustic soda and cane sugar are raw materials made using fairly standardized processes. Oils and glycerin on the other hand come from different sources all around the world, and are refined with differing processes. So contamination will most likely occur in oils or glycerin. To find out which one you can either purchase raw materials from another source or substitute ingredients until you isolate the problem. Tallow, lard or stearic acid can substitute for palm oil, palm kernel can replace coconut. Extra sugar solution can be used instead of glycerin.

One final note: Cloudiness can sometimes appear in the liquid soap stock even after the soap has completely dissolved in alcohol. Test the pH – *the cloudiness is probably due to an excess or deficiency of lye.* Correct for this using the procedure outlined in Section 5-c. *Contaminated ingredients could also cause this problem.*

Problem:
6) SOAP DOESN'T HARDEN IN MOLDS

Solution:

> **Your soap should take no longer than 12 hours to firm up, but if it hasn't within this time, give it another day or so.**

None of the recipes in this book will have difficulty setting. If any do, perhaps you've over-added solvents while trying to correct for cloudiness, or maybe you've mismeasured ingredients. If the soap hasn't firmed up after 24 hours in the mold, you could try remelting it

continued on next page . . .

then adding a few ounces of melted stearic acid and lye to act as a hardener. *See Section 5-b above for the procedure on adding extra stearic acid and lye.*

Problem:

7) STICKY, CLOUDY TOP LAYER

Solution:

If your hardened bars have a sticky, cloudy layer on top and a clear, firm transparent layer beneath, your soap has either an excess of oil or a deficiency of lye.

> **You can try remelting this kind of soap and adding a bit more lye solution. Follow the instructions given in Section 5-c above. If the layer isn't too thick, the addition of extra lye will probably eliminate it.**

Don't expect as much success with thicker and more pronounced layering. If corrective measures don't solve the problem, skim off the sticky layer – it can always be used to wash dishes.

Appendices

A SHORT HISTORY OF SOAPMAKING

Soapmaking is one of the oldest industries in the world although no one really knows just when soap was discovered. The first reference to soap occurs in Sumerian clay tablets dating around 2500 B.C., but this was probably not a true soap. The early Romans used hot water and scraped their bodies with twigs or a special tool called a "strigil." Some sources indicate that the Gauls were the first people to make soap and that the later Romans, during the conquests of Julius Caesar, learned the art from them. Excavations of ancient Pompeii reveal the presence of a soap factory.

Soap manufacture flourished in Europe from the eighth century onwards in such towns as Castilla in Spain, Marseilles in France and Savona in Italy. The city name of Savona is the source for the names "savon," "sabon," and "jabon," which means soap in French, Portuguese and Spanish respectively. These earlier soaps were only available to the rich; it wasn't until the 19th century that decent quality soap could be afforded by the common person.

Probably the first and certainly the most well-known of transparent soap is Pears brand. In 1798, Andrew Pears opened a barber shop in a fashionable London neighborhood. As business grew, he began making his own creams, pomades and powders. The soaps available at that time were often crude and quite alkaline, and so Pears set about experimenting with his own formulas. He discovered that by dissolving ordinary soap in alcohol the resulting soap was both mild and transparent. Mass-production began and with the promotional help of his son-in-law Thomas J. Barratt, often called the Father of Advertising, Pears created a market which still retains a loyal following some 200 years later.

RENDERING TALLOW

If you haven't any philosophical objections to animal-based soap, you can use either lard, which is found in one-pound blocks at your grocery, or you can render tallow. Rendering needs to be done a day before soapmaking.

Tallow can be purchased from butchers or rendering plants. It usually comes in large slabs, though some butchers grind it up into hamburger consistency for customers with bird feeders. Hamburger consistency is ideal; the smaller the pieces, the faster the rendering time. Buy more fat than what the recipe calls for since there are some impurities which will be discarded after rendering. If a recipe calls for two pounds of tallow, buy three. And as long as you're going through the trouble of rendering, make some extra now if you'll be mixing more soap in the future. It keeps indefinitely in the freezer.

To render, chop the tallow into small chunks. In a large pot, bring to a boil a few cups of water. (Some opaque soapmaking books call for salted water. Salt can cause cloudiness in transparent soap.) Toss the fat in. Stirring occasionally, bring the water back up to a boil then turn the heat to low and cover the pot. Depending on the amount of fat being rendered, it could take a few hours until all the fat has melted. If you're impatient, the process can be expedited by chopping up the hot chunks of fat in a blender or food processor.

Once the fat has completely melted, pour it through a large strainer and into another pot or bowl; toss out any of the impurities that might be left in the strainer. Let the fat cool to room temperature then set in the refrigerator overnight. By the next day, the fat will have cooled into three layers – white tallow on top, a middle

continued on next page . . .

. . . continued from previous page

greyish granular layer, and water or gel on the bottom. Lift up the disc of tallow and scrape away all of the grey layer adhering to it.

This disc of white tallow will soon be transformed into a clear, jewel-like bar of transparent soap.

USING PHENOLPHTHALEIN

The chemical phenolphthalein has wide and oddly diverse uses. It's used as a laxative, as a component in dye manufacture, and most importantly for the soapmaker, it functions as an acid-base indicator. I find it far more useful than pH strips. Phenolphthalein doesn't give a numerical value to the pH, as strips will do, but pH strips can be hard to read. A digital pH meter with an electrolyte probe is the ideal tool for an accurate pH reading, but these are expensive.

Phenolphthalein can be purchased as either a colorless liquid or a powder which can be dissolved in water or alcohol. Phenolphthalein will turn pink or red in the presence of an alkali and remain clear in the presence of an acid. A pH of 7 (the value of water) is considered truly neutral. All pH values from 1 to 6.9 are acids, the value 1 being the most acidic. From the pH 7.1 up to pH 14, the values are increasingly alkaline.

This can be somewhat confusing when applied to soapmaking. "Neutral" soap is not neutral in the sense of a pH of 7. Neutral soap is quite alkaline, with a pH of around 9.5. But soap is considered neutral if it contains no excess of either fatty acids or alkalis. So when a drop of phenolphthalein is applied to a sample of soap, the appearance of a pink color does not indicate a pH which is 7.1 or above. It indicates a pH above 9.5, or a soap which contains unsaponified caustic soda. A drop of phenolphthalein which remains clear when applied to soap indicates that the soap's pH is 9.5 or below. If below 9.5, unsaponified fatty acids are present in the soap, which is fine to a point; many commercial soaps are "superfatted" with excess acids in order to create a creamier, milder soap. But if the pH is too low, if there is too much unsaponified oil in the soap, both opaque and transparent bars will be too soft to use. And in the case of transparent soap particularly, excess fatty acids can cause cloudiness.

To use phenolphthalein, squeeze a drop directly onto a sample of soap after it's been through the gel stage. If a pink color appears, the soap contains excess caustic soda; the deeper the pink, the more the excess. Cover the soap and allow more time for neutralization. If it still tests pink after another half hour to hour, add glycerin and alcohol and proceed with mixing. Now correct the pH using the technique given in Section 5-c of the Troubleshooting chapter. Add stearic acid a little at a time until the pink disappears.

If the phenolphthalein remains clear when dropped onto a sample of soap, the pH will be at 9.5 or below. If the soap appears good – i.e., it's clear and hardens well, doesn't seem soft and greasy when a finger is pressed into a hardened sample – leave it alone. But if the phenolphthalein remains clear when dropped onto a sample that's cloudy and feels greasy when a finger is pressed into a hardened sample, try adding more lye solution. Again, use the technique given in Section 5-c of the Troubleshooting chapter. Add lye solution a little at a time, mix for 20 minutes then test. Continue until

continued on next page . . .

. . . continued from previous page

the phenolphthalein registers the faintest shade of pink when dropped onto a sample, then stop. Settle the soap then pour into molds.

FORMULATING YOUR OWN OPAQUE AND TRANSPARENT SOAP

This appendix will give you all the basic information you need for formulating either opaque or transparent soap from a descriptive approach. Soapmaking can be approached more scientifically using saponification numbers, iodine numbers, etc. This information can be found in soapmaking manuals in the reserve section of your local library.

a. Choosing Your Oils

First become familiar with the soapmaking properties of the basic oils. Chapter 2 and the information contained in this appendix should be sufficient. Then decide upon a blend – this is both an art and a matter of personal preference.

Many commercial opaque soaps are approximately 80-90% tallow or palm and 10-20% coconut. A formulation can be that simple. The addition of a soft oil will give more of a cold-cream finish to soap, so a revised formulation could be 70% tallow or palm, 20% coconut and 10% of a soft oil. Just remember that soap will lose firmness as larger percentages of soft oils are added.

More variables exist with transparent soap. The oils need to be blended with a little extra care, because blends which are suitable for opaque soap don't always work with transparent. For example, a high percentage of coconut oil is fine in opaque soap but too large a percentage in transparent causes cloudiness. Then there are the solvents to consider. Solvents, as well as oils, have their own characteristics. A proper balance must also be struck between the solvents and the oil blend. Below are some general parameters to keep in mind when blending oils. Section c in this appendix will give some guidelines for the solvents.

1. Palm Oil or Tallow. These oils form the base of both opaque and transparent soap. Either oil can account for between 30-75% of the total for the oil blend. I personally keep the percentages at around 50-60%.

2. Coconut Oil. Too much coconut oil in a formulation clouds the transparency. Between 10-35% of the oil blend can consist of coconut or palm kernel oil.

3. Castor Oil. This oil imparts exceptional clarity, but an excess creates a soft, poor-lathering soap. 15-35% is a good range for castor. Remember that the more castor you use, the smaller the proportion of alcohol you'll need to dissolve the soap due to castor's solvent-like properties.

4. Rosin. Like castor oil, it's both a solvent and a saponifiable oil. Rosin imparts even more clarity than castor, but it also creates more softness and stickiness. Keep the percentages a little lower than castor – 5-20% of an oil blend. You might try adding stearic acid to counteract rosin's softening effect, especially when formulating with higher percentages of rosin. Too much sugar in a rosin soap causes efflorescence, so take care with sugar. This will be discussed in Section c.

continued on next page . . .

. . . continued from previous page

b. Calculating the Caustic Soda Solution

After deciding upon a blend, the next step is to calculate how much caustic soda is required to saponify the given amount of oil. Chart #2 at the end of the appendix gives the percentage of dry soda (not solution) needed for each oil. Notice the range in percentages for each oil. Fatty acid contents can vary according to how the oil is refined, how old the oil is (acid content tends to rise the older the oil), and even the price of oil on the world market. When the price of coconut rises too high, it's often blended with less-expensive palm kernel oil, which greatly affects coconut oil's fatty acid content. When formulating, choose a middle percentage between the two extremes for each oil.

Assume you formulate a recipe using 2 pounds palm, 2 pounds coconut and 1.25 pounds of castor oil. Refer to the chart. It takes approximately 14.3% dry caustic soda to saponify a given amount of palm. Convert the 2 pounds palm into ounces (32) and multiply by .143. You need 4.5 ounces caustic soda to neutralize the palm. Use the same math for the coconut and castor. Coconut requires .183 ounces caustic x 32 ounces oil, or 5.9 ounces caustic. Multiply .13 x 20 ounces of castor for 2.6 ounces caustic. Add these 3 numbers up and the total amount of caustic soda will be 13 ounces.

For the water portion of the soda solution, all the recipes in this book have been calculated using a fairly standard strength lye solution – 32.5% caustic soda to 67.5% water. Dividing 67.5 by 32.5 equals 2.08. That's the constant you'll use for the soda/water solutions. If you multiply 13 ounces of dry caustic soda by 2.08, you'll need 27 ounces of water (or a total of 40 ounces lye solution).

c. Solvents

Transparent soapmakers now need to calculate the proportions of alcohol, glycerin and sugar solution. Below are some general parameters for these ingredients. Keep in mind that these numbers as well as those for the oils aren't iron-clad rules. Straying a few percentage points in either direction won't ruin your soap. But they do offer a good starting place and give some insight into the balance necessary for successful transparent soap.

1. Alcohol. This is the primary solvent for all transparent soap. Multiply the total weight of actual soap by 30-35% for the weight a formulation needs in alcohol. Actual soap is the weight of the oils and dry caustic soda. The water in the lye solution is counted as a solvent, not part of the actual soap. For example, if you have a formulation requiring 80 ounces of oil and 12 ounces of caustic soda beads, the weight of actual soap is 92 ounces. 92 x .30 or .35 = 28 to 32 ounces of alcohol necessary to dissolve the soap. Remember, the more castor oil or rosin in the oil blend, the less alcohol is necessary.

2. Water. Water should account for approximately 12-20% of the formulation's weight. This includes the water in both the lye and sugar solutions.

3. Glycerin. Excellent for transparency, but too much causes softness and sweating. 8-12% glycerin per total weight of the formulation is a good parameter. Glycerin can be replaced partially or completely by extra sugar solution.

4. Sugar. Similar to glycerin, but even better at producing transparency ounce per ounce. Too much causes softness,

continued on next page . . .

. . . continued from previous page

stickiness and even efflorescence. Try to keep the total proportion of sugar (dry, not the total weight of the solution) at around 6-9% of the recipe. If you're formulating without glycerin, sugar can account for up to 13-14% of the total.

Transparent soap consists of approximately 50-60% actual soap to 40-50% solvent. When formulating a recipe, first calculate the oils and caustic soda proportions. From these numbers find the weight of actual soap. Then take this number and calculate the recipe in two ways: one at 60% soap to 40% solvent, the other at 50% soap to 50% solvent.

Make the soap. Then add the amount of solvents called for in the 40% formulation. After adding sugar and testing for transparency, evaluate the hardened sample. If it lacks a good transparency, refer to your 50/50 soap to solvent formulation. Using simple subtraction, calculate how much more of each solvent the 40% mixture will require to bring it up to the 50/50 mixture. Weigh each of the solvents and begin adding them to the 60/40 solution a few ounces at a time, testing on glass after each addition. If a good transparency is achieved at 55% soap to 45% solvent, stop there. More is not better. More is softer. Then weigh what's left of each remaining solvent. Extrapolate from this figure just how much was added to the 40% solution. These additional ounces plus the numbers of the 40% solution become your recipe.

Confused? Let's apply these principals to the formulation from Section b: 2 pounds tallow or palm, 2 pounds coconut, 1 pound 4 ounces castor oil and 13 ounces of dry caustic soda. This totals 97 ounces actual soap. For the 40% solvent number, multiply 97 by .8, or 77 ounces of solvent. (Use .8 for all 40% solvent calculations.)

THE RECIPE AT 40% MIGHT LOOK SOMETHING LIKE THIS:

Actual Soap	Solvents
2 pounds palm	1 pound 11 ounces water (in lye solution)
2 pounds coconut	1 pound 13 ounces alcohol (97 x .30)
1 pound 4 ounces castor	1 pound glycerin
13 ounces caustic soda	5 ounces water (in sugar solution)
= 97 ounces actual soap	= 77 ounces solvents

97 ounces actual soap plus 77 ounces of solvent equals 174 ounces. For the amount of sugar you'll need, multiply 174 times .07 or .08. This equals approximately 13 ounces. Add this number to 174 ounces and your total recipe will weigh 187 ounces. Of that, water accounts for 17%, glycerin for 8.5% and sugar for 7.5%.

THE RECIPE AT 50% MIGHT LOOK SOMETHING LIKE THIS:

You'll need 97 ounces of solvents, which is 20 ounces more than the total solvents needed for the 60/40 formulation.

Actual Soap	Solvents
2 pounds palm	1 pound 11 ounces water (in lye solution)
2 pounds coconut	2 pounds 2 ounces alcohol (97 x .35)
1 pound 4 ounces castor	1 pound 5 ounces glycerin
13 ounces caustic soda	15 ounces water (in sugar solution)
= 97 ounces actual soap	= 97 ounces solvents

97 ounces soap plus 97 ounces solvent equals 194. Multiply 194 by .07 or .08 and you'll need approximately 1 pound of sugar. The total recipe now weighs 210 ounces. Of that, water accounts for 20%, glycerin for 10% and sugar about 7.5%.

So if the transparency isn't satisfactory at 60/40, you have another 20 ounces of solvent to add before a 50/50 blend is

continued on next page . . .

. . . continued from previous page

created. These 20 ounces consist of an additional 5 ounces alcohol, 5 ounces glycerin, and 10 ounces water. I usually withhold 3 or 4 ounces of the water just in case the transparency isn't quite right at 50/50. I then add a few ounces of extra sugar to this remaining water and try to get the proper clarity without having to add extra liquid.

I'm very conservative when formulating a recipe containing rosin, especially with the percentages of sugar. I start with sugar accounting for approximately 3-4% of the total. Soap without rosin is generally forgiving of excesses in sugar; soap containing larger percentages of rosin is not.

A final note if you want to increase or decrease any of the recipes in this book: I strongly recommend using the procedure outlined above for a 60/40 and 50/50 mix. When doubling or tripling a recipe, I've occasionally noticed that less solvent is necessary. If you want to decrease a recipe, please use the double-boiler method outlined on page 38. A smaller mass of soap will generate less heat in the gel stage – this soap may not neutralize properly. The double-boiler method provides an external heat source to compensate for the loss of chemical heat.

CHART #1: SOAPMAKING PROPERTIES OF COMMON OILS AND FATS

Soap Made From	Color	Consistency	Lather	Cleansing Properties	Action on Skin	How Saponified
Coconut Oil	Pale yellow to white	Extremely hard	Quick, foamy, large bubbles – does not last	Excellent	Biting action; roughens skin	Quickly
Palm Kernel Oil	Pale yellow to white	Extremely hard	Quick, foamy, large bubbles – does not last	Excellent	Biting action; roughens skin	Quickly
Palm Oil	Buff	Very hard	Slow, lasting, close	Very good	Very mild	Very easily
Tallow	Pale buff to white	Very hard	Fairly slow, lasting, thick	Good	Very mild	Fairly easily
Lard	White	Hard	Fairly slow, lasting, thick	Good	Very mild	Fairly easily
Castor Oil	Pale yellow	Soft	Thick, lasting	Fair	Mild	Easily
Olive Oil	Various shades green	Very soft	Oily, close, lather persists	Very fair	Very mild	Fairly easily
Rosin	Yellow to dark brown	Soft	Oily, thick	Fair	Mild	Quickly
Cottonseed Oil	Buff to bright yellow	Medium to soft	Oily, abundant, medium lasting	Good	Mild	Fairly easily
Soybean Oil	Pale yellow to dull white	Soft	Oily, abundant, medium lasting	Fair	Mild	Fairly easily

Chart #2:

Percentage Dry Sodium Hydroxide Necessary to Saponify Common Oils, Fats and Fatty Acids

Coconut Oil	17.9-18.8 %
Palm Kernel Oil	15.3-15.6 %
Palm Oil	14-14.6 %
Tallow	13.8-14.3 %
Lard	13.6-14 %
Castor Oil	12.8-13.2 %
Olive Oil	13.5-14 %
Rosin	12.1-13.8 %
Corn Oil	13.2-13.8 %
Cottonseed Oil	13.6-14%
Soybean Oil	13.4-13.6 %
Stearic Acid	13.75-14.25%
Oleic Acid	13.5-14%

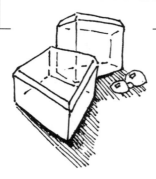

THE ALCOHOL/LYE METHOD OF
TRANSPARENT SOAPMAKING

There's an alternative to part of the transparent soapmaking methodology outlined in this book. I'll call it the Alcohol/Lye Method, and it eliminates the 2-hour gel time. Using this alternative technique, the soapmaker runs the alcohol as well as the lye solution into the oil blend and stirs. The presence of alcohol greatly increases the saponification rate. There's no resting phase to the soap, just continual stirring.

I've tried this method and it works well. So why didn't I use it for the book since it saves time and eliminates a procedure? Two reasons. First, soap made using the alcohol/lye method is less neutral than soap which passes through the gel stage. Free alkali remains. And second, I designed this book so that as little time as possible is spent in handling alcohol. The alcohol/lye method involves a mixing time of 1-1/2 to 2 hours, much longer than is necessary for gel-phase transparent soap. So not only is there more likelihood for evaporation (leading to cloudy soap) but there's also that much more time spent worrying about fire hazards.

This is not to discourage anyone from trying this method – it is a viable alternative sometimes used by transparent soapmakers. If you do use it, it's extremely important to become familiar not only with the fire hazards of alcohol use, but also the precautionary measures necessary for setting up your kitchen or workspace. Chapter 4 outlines this information.

continued on next page . . .

. . . continued from previous page

The procedure for the alcohol/lye method is as follows: Add room-temperature alcohol to the 135-145 degree F. lye solution. Stir both into the 135-145 degree oil blend. Cover this broth with plastic tenting or the variable-speed mixer jig and place over medium heat. Begin stirring. Raise the temperature to 160 degrees F. and stir continuously for 1-1/2 to 2 hours. Check the temperature occasionally; it if falls much below 160, gently warm the broth back up.

After 1-1/2 or 2 hours, stop mixing. The soap will not be completely neutral, so have some melted stearic acid ready. If you have phenolphthalein, use it. It should take between one and two ounces of stearic acid to neutralize the soap stock. Stir again for another 20 minutes to ensure the thorough incorporation of the stearic acid.

Add the glycerin and sugar solution, stir for a minute, then let the soap settle for 20 minutes. Add the color and fragrance and pour into molds.

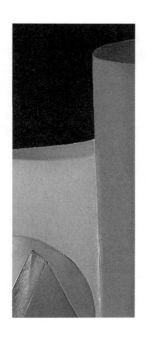

Glossary

Alkali. Any base or hydroxide soluble in water and able to neutralize acids. In soapmaking, sodium or potassium hydroxide neutralizes fatty acids.

Cold-process. A soapmaking technique which relies almost exclusively on the heat generated by the chemical reaction of fatty acids and alkali to produce soap. No external heat is applied once the ingredients have been mixed.

Colloid. A gel-like substance made up of very small, insoluble particles larger than molecules but small enough so that they remain suspended in a fluid medium. All soap exists in a colloidal state during part of saponification. Transparent soap is soap held in this colloidal state through the addition of certain solvents such as alcohol and glycerin.

Distilled water. Water which has been boiled then condensed to remove any mineral or other impurities.

Efflorescence. A term used in transparent soapmaking to describe a milkiness or gradual clouding of the soap's transparency.

Essential Oil. A volatile oil steamed or pressed from the fruits, flowers, stems or roots of plants. Used especially for perfumes, soaps and flavorings.

Ethanol, or ethyl alcohol. Clear, colorless and very flammable. Produced from the fermentation of carbohydrates, it's the primary alcohol used in the production of transparent soap.

Fatty Acid. Along with glycerides, fatty acids are the main constituents of animal and vegetable fats. Fatty acids are what react chemically with the alkalis to form soap. There are many kinds of fatty acids, and each has distinct properties which in turn affect the characteristics of the soap produced from them.

Fragrance Oil. A laboratory-produced synthetic version of a true essential oil or a natural fragrance, such as peach. Often fragrance oils are a combination of both synthetic and true essential oils.

Full-boiled. A soapmaking process in which the oils and caustic solution are combined then heated in steam kettles to the boiling point. This allows for the most complete neutralization of free fatty acids and alkalis, and is the process used by large-scale soap manufacturers.

Glycerin. A thick, sweet-tasting clear fluid that's actually an alcohol. A by-product of soap manufacture, it can also be produced synthetically from propylene, a petroleum by-product. Used as an emollient, humectant and as a primary solvent in the manufacture of transparent soaps.

Hard Fat. Any animal or vegetable fat which is solid at room temperature; largely composed of the fatty acids stearin and palmitin. Palm oil and tallow are the two most common hard fats used for soapmaking.

Humectant. A substance used to preserve moisture content. The humectant glycerin combined with rose water is the earliest known lotion.

Isopropyl alcohol. A petroleum-derived alcohol sometimes used as a partial substitute for ethyl alcohol in transparent soapmaking.

pH. Standing for the "potential of hydrogen," it's a term used to indicate acidity or alkalinity. A pH of 7, or the value of pure water, is regarded as neutral. Acids have a pH below 7, alkalis above 7. "Neutral" soap, however, is approximately a pH of 9.5, or alkaline.

Phenolphthalein. A chemical compound used as an acid-base indicator, turning pink in the presence of an alkali and remaining colorless in a solution containing acid.

Potassium hydroxide. Also known as caustic potash. A strong alkali; when combined with a fatty acid it produces liquid soap.

Rendering. The process by which tallow (beef fat) is boiled in water to remove the impurities. The cleaned fat is then used for soapmaking.

Rosin. The pale-yellow residue remaining after the volatile oils are distilled from the oleoresin of pine trees. Rosin acts as a preservative and greatly enhances the transparency of the soap.

Saponification. The chemical reaction which converts a fatty acid and an alkali into soap and glycerin.

Semi-boiled. One of three basic soapmaking processes. Oils and a caustic solution are mixed then heated to between 140-160 degrees F. Transparent soap is made using the semi-boiled method.

Soap. Along with glycerin, soap is the by-product of a chemical reaction involving fatty acids and caustic soda or potash. Soap is actually a salt.

Sodium Hydroxide. Also known as caustic soda, it's one of two primary alkalis used in the production of soap. Combined with a fatty acid it produces a hard soap.

Soft Oils. Liquid at room temperature, most soft oils are characterized by a high percentage of the unsaturated fatty acids oleic and linoleic. Olive, canola, cottonseed are soft oils. Castor is the soft oil of choice for transparent soap-making due to its ability to act as a solvent. It is characterized by a high percentage of ricinoleic acid.

Solvent. A liquid capable of dissolving or dispersing another substance. Alcohol, glycerin, water and sugar solutions are all solvents used to hold soap in a colloidal state for the purpose of rendering opaque soap transparent.

Transparency. Soap is officially termed transparent if 14-point typeface can be read clearly through a 1/4" thick slice of soap.

Source Books and Suppliers of Raw Materials

SOURCE BOOKS FOR RAW MATERIALS

Most of the materials necessary for transparent soapmaking can usually be found in your local area. If not, here is a list of suppliers. These suppliers can also sell larger quantities (therefore cheaper per pound) than you might find locally.

Besides the suppliers listed below, another excellent source of information is the **Thomas Register**. Most any library will have this extensive, multi-volume guide in its reference section. The **Register** contains a national listing of sources for almost anything imaginable – from nuts and bolts to castor oil, essential oils, etc. Some of these businesses won't sell in small quantities, but some will.

Buyer's guides are also available through trade publications. Again, many of the companies listed sell in quantity to manufacturers only. Here are two guides.

Blue Book
Soap Cosmetics Chemical Specialties
445 Broad Hollow Rd.
Melville, NY 11747
516-845-2700

DCI Directory Issue
Advanstar Communications
Attn: Marketing Service
131 W. 1st St
Duluth, MN 55802
1-800-346-0085

SUPPLIERS OF RAW MATERIALS

CASTOR OIL
- Chem Lab Supplies
- Frontier Cooperative Herbs
- Janca's Jojoba Oil and Seed Co.
- Liberty Natural Products
- Penta Manufacturing Co.

COCONUT OIL
- Chem Lab Supplies
- Essential Oil Company
- Janca's Jojoba Oil and Seed Co.
- Liberty Natural Products
- Penta Manufacturing Co.
- Shay & Company
- Uncommon Scents

SUPPLIERS OF RAW MATERIALS

ESSENTIAL OILS
- Aphrodisia Products Inc.
- Aromatica
- Escential Lotions and Oils
- Essential Oil Co.
- Frontier Cooperative Herbs
- Indiana Botanical Gardens
- Janca's Jojoba Oil and Seed Co.
- Liberty Natural Products
- Nectarine
- Penta Manufacturing Co.
- Uncommon Scents

ETHANOL (Denatured)
- Chem Lab Supplies
- HPC Scientific & Technology
- Nurnberg Scientific

FRAGRANCE OILS
- Aphrodisia Products Inc.
- Aromatica
- Escential Lotions and Oils
- Essential Oil Co.
- Frontier Cooperative Herbs
- Janca's Jojoba Oil and Seed Co.
- Nectarine
- Penta Manufacturing Co.
- Uncommon Scents

GLYCERIN
- Aphrodisia Products Inc.
- Carolina Biological Supply Co.
- Chem Lab Supplies
- Essential Oil Co.
- Frontier Cooperative Herbs
- Janca's Jojoba Oil and Seed Co.
- Liberty Natural Products
- Nurnberg Scientific
- Penta Manufacturing Co.

MOLDS
- Barker Enterprises, Inc.
- Georgie's Ceramics and Clay
- Pourette Manufacturing Co.

MUSIC WIRE
- McMaster-Carr Supply Co.
- Wink's Hardware

PALM OIL
- Chem Lab Supplies
- Essential Oil Co.
- Frontier Cooperative Herbs
- Janca's Jojoba Oil and Seed Co.
- Liberty Natural Products
- Penta Manufacturing Co.
- Shay & Company

PHENOLPHTHALEIN
- Carolina Biological Supply Co.
- Chem Lab Supplies
- HPC Scientific & Technology
- Nurnberg Scientific
- Penta Manufacturing Co.

PRESERVATIVES
- Chem Lab Supplies
- Frontier Cooperative Herbs
- Janca's Jojoba Oil and Seed Co.
- Liberty Natural Products

ROSIN
- Chem Lab Supplies
- Nurnberg Scientific
- Dabney Herbs
- Woodworker's Supply

SOAP DYES
- Georgie's Ceramic and Clay
- Pourette Manufacturing Co.

SUPPLIERS OF RAW MATERIALS

SODIUM HYDROXIDE
- Chem Lab Supplies
- Janca's Jojoba Oil and Seed Co.
- HPC Scientific & Technology
- Nurnberg Scientific
- Penta Manufacturing Co.

STEARIC ACID
- Barker Enterprises, Inc.
- Carolina Biological Supply Co.
- Chem Lab Supplies
- Georgie's Ceramics and Clay
- HPC Scientific&Technology
- Liberty Natural Products
- Nurnberg Scientific
- Penta Manufacturing Co.
- Pourette Manufacturing Co.

TALLOW
- George Pfau's Sons Company, Inc.
- Stevenson-Cooper, Inc.
- Welch, Holmes & Clark Co., Inc.

SUPPLIERS' ADDRESSES

Aphrodisia
264 Bleeker Street
New York, NY 10014
212-989-6440

Aromatica
513 N. 36th Street
Seattle, WA 98103
206-545-8100

SUPPLIERS' ADDRESSES

Barker Enterprises, Inc.
15106-10th Avenue SW
Seattle, WA 98166
800-543-0601

Carolina Biological Supply Co.
2700 York Rd.
Burlington, NC 272115
910-584-03381

Chem Lab Supplies
1060 Ortega Way, Unit C
Placentia, CA 92670
714-630-7902

Dabney Herbs
P.O. Box 22061
Louisville, KY 40252
502-893-5198

Escential Lotions and Oils
710 NW 23rd Avenue
Portland, OR 97210
503-248-9748

Essential Oil Co.
P.O. Box 206
Lake Oswego, OR 97034
800-729-5912

Frontier Cooperative Herbs
3021 78th Street
P.O. Box 299
Norway, IA 52318
800-669-3275

George Pfau's Sons Company, Inc.
P.O. Box 7
Jeffersonville, IN 47131-0007
800-732-8645

SUPPLIERS' ADDRESSES

Georgie's Ceramics and Clay Co.
756 NE Lombard
Portland, OR 97211
800-999-2529

HPC Scientific&Technology
P.O. Box 17376
Portland, OR 97217
503-249-2985

Indiana Botanic Gardens Inc.
3401 W. 37th Avenue
Hobart, IN 46342
219-947-4040

Janca's Jojoba Oil and Seed Co.
456 E. Juanita #7
Mesa, AZ 85204
602-497-9494

Liberty Natural Products
8120 SE Stark Street
Portland, OR 97215
800-289-8427

McMaster-Carr Supply Co.
P.O. Box 4355
Chicago, IL 60680-4355
630-834-9600

Nectarine
1200 Fifth Street
Berkeley, CA 94710
510-528-0162

Nurnberg Scientific
6310 S.W. Virginia Avenue
Portland, OR 97201
800-826-3470

Penta Manufacturing Co.
P.O. Box 1448
Fairfield, NJ 07007
201-740-2300

Pourette Manufacturing Co.
P.O. Box 17056
Seattle, WA 98107
800-888-9425

Shay & Company
8535 N. Lombard, #202
Portland, OR 97203
503-289-5503

Stevenson-Cooper, Inc.
P.O. Box 38349
Philadelphia, PA 19140
215-223-2600

Uncommon Scents
P.O. Box 1941
Eugene, OR 97440
800-426-4336

Welch, Holme & Clark Co., Inc.
#7 Avenue L
Newark, NJ 07105
201-465-1200

Wink's Hardware
P.O. Box 6055
Portland, OR 97228
503-227-5536

Woodworker's Supply
1108 North Glenn Road
Casper, WY 82601
800-645-9292

BIBLIOGRAPHY

Davidsohn, Better and Davidsohn, **Soap Manufacture, Volume 1.** New York: Interscience Publishers, Inc., 1953.

Gathmann, Henry, **American Soaps**. Chicago: Henry Gathmann, 1893.

Kuntom, Ainie, et. al., ''Transparent/Translucent Soap Derived From Palm Oil.'' Paper read at the ABISA Congress, October 1992, Olinda, Brazil.

Osteroth, David, ''Transparent Soaps.'' *Dragoco Report* (November/December, 1979).

Thomssen, E.G., and Kemp, C.R., **Modern Soap Making**. MacNair-Dorland Co., 1937.

Whalley, George, ''See-Through Soaps.'' *HAPPI* (July, 1993).

Index

A PERSONAL POSTSCRIPT:
Hard work, patient observation and a real love for transparent soapmaking enabled me to write this book. I only hope that I have communicated my knowledge clearly enough so that readers can experience both success with transparent soapmaking and the incredible aesthetic pleasure that comes from creating something beautiful. I'd also love to hear from anyone with further information pertaining to transparent soapmaking.

ABOUT THE AUTHOR
Catherine Failor was an amateur soapmaker for 13 years before founding Copra Soap. Drawing from a background in art and design, she created a whole new look in bar soap. For the past 7 years Copra Soap has been manufacturing a wide variety of soap inlaid with colorful patterns – polka dots, checkerboards, rainbow stripes, stars, etc. These soaps have been sold in stores across the country and overseas. Gift catalogues such as Eddie Bauer, Norm Thompson and Tweeds have also featured these unique bars. Catherine lives in Portland, Oregon.

Questions about soap?

Catherine offers a telephone consulting service for anyone with questions pertaining to all aspects of opaque or transparent soapmaking. The charge for this service is $60 an hour, billed by the minute to your Visa or Mastercard.

For information on Copra Soap's product line, or to order soap molds designed by Catherine, call 503-771-3234.

Rose City Press
4326 SE Woodstock Blvd, Suite 374
Portland, OR 97206
Telephone: (503) 771-3234